The Call to Care

The Call to Care

Essays by
Unitarian Universalist Chaplains

KAREN L. HUTT
Editor

Skinner House Books
Boston

www.skinnerhouse.org

Printed in the United States

Cover and text design by Suzanne Morgan
Cover photo by Nikki Zalewski/Shutterstock
Author photo by Steve Rouch

print ISBN: 978-1-55896-785-4
eBook ISBN: 978-1-55896-786-1

6 5 4 3 2 1
19 18 17 16

Library of Congress Cataloging-in-Publication Data
Names: Hutt, Karen L., 1958- author.
Title: The call to care : essays by Unitarian Universalist chaplains / Karen
   L. Hutt.
Description: Boston : Skinner House Books, 2016. | Includes bibliographical
   references.
Identifiers: LCCN 2016033729 | ISBN 9781558967854 (pbk. : alk. paper)
Subjects: LCSH: Church work with the sick. | Pastoral care. | Medical
   care--Religious aspects. | Unitarian Universalist churches. | Unitarian
   Universalist Association--Doctrines.
Classification: LCC BV4335 .H88 2016 | DDC 253/.391--dc23 LC record avail-
able at https://lccn.loc.gov/2016033729

We gratefully acknowledge permission to reprint the following:
"Out beyond ideas of wrongdoing . . ." by Jalal al-Din Rumi, trans. by Coleman
Barks, from The Essential Rumi copyright © 1995 by Coleman Barks, reprinted
by permission of Coleman Barks; selected lyrics from "Come, Sing a Song with
Me" by Carolyn McDade, © 1976 Surtsey Publishing, renewed © 1992 by
Carolyn McDade, reprinted by permission of Carolyn McDade.

Contents

Foreword

When I entered seminary in 1996, coming straight from the corporate world, I wasn't sure what kind of ministry I had been called to. The pull to give my life in service to something bigger than myself—whether that was God, a religious community, and/or the greater good—was so strong that I did not know, or much care, where it would ultimately lead me.

My seminary studies, my internship in a congregation, and my Clinical Pastoral Education in a hospital led me to the path of parish ministry. For ten years I did the things that parish ministers do—preach, pastor, manage, administer, fundraise, march, and learn. I enjoyed the work and then I was called to a new type of ministry when I became the founding executive director of the Unitarian Universalist Ministers Association. My new ministry invited me to do much of what I had learned in the parish and added new challenges as well. Not long after I began my new work, I became intimately aware of the biases and judgments our culture and our faith have toward those who minister in communities rather than parishes.

It's rare in our culture to see examples of ministers in non-congregational settings. I'm not sure exactly how long it was after I left the parish—but it wasn't long—when I talked about my ministry and my wife and son said, "You are not a minister anymore, you are an executive director." I protested, and we eventually laughed. But too often when I hear colleagues

and others speak about ministers, they leave out those who are
ministering in places other than congregations. Community
ministers, as we call those of us not serving in congregations,
represent the fastest-growing form of ministry in our faith these
days. Almost 25 percent of our active ministers identify this way.
And chaplains are a major portion of community ministers.

In ancient times, the word *ministry* meant to serve. Universalist minister Gordon McKeeman claimed that ministry
is a quality of relationship between and among human beings
that beckons forth hidden possibilities and invites people into
deeper, more constant, more reverent relationship with the
world and one another. If we hold his words and the original
definition of ministry to be true, to minister means to serve and
bring forth the best in each other.

This collection of essays on chaplaincy provides examples
of ministers serving and bringing forth the best in each other.
These stories bring us to places where pain and isolation are
often the most prevalent—prisons, hospital rooms, recovery
centers, and battlefields. These testimonies about the joys and
challenges of being present for another person, particularly
when they may be different in culture, race, class or religious
faith, remind us of the best of our Unitarian Universalist faith.

The first Principle of Unitarian Universalism states that we
affirm and promote the inherent worth and dignity of every
person. The hard reality of living this out is one of the biggest
challenges we face. These essays remind me not only how difficult this can be but also why it is so central to our faith and to
ministry. Time and time again my colleagues describe the skills
and wisdom they have learned in order to be outstanding chaplains. They also share where they get the strength and inspiration to be with people in their most vulnerable and scary times.
Sometimes the source is God, sometimes it is love, sometimes
it is their faith, always it is their deep commitment and call to
minister and to be with another human being.

When I spent ten months doing my Clinical Pastoral Education in a hospital as part of my ministerial training, there
wasn't a book like this one to teach and inspire me in my work.
I learned, often through trial and error, how to offer that most

precious gift, the gift of presence, when we sit with another person, offering our heart, our ears, and our humanity, without judgment or expectation.

My colleagues in this book have not only learned this gift but are offering it to each of us so that we might remember how to not only practice our faith but to live our lives. Even if we have not spent time in prison, the throes of addiction, an army battalion, or a hospital emergency room, we know others who have and we know the heartbreak and fear that life often provides. These stories show us that in the midst of our bleakest days we have the chance to offer ourselves to another and to invite others to do the same.

These chaplains, these ministers, may not preach every Sunday but they offer us a sermon we should never forget—the call to care.

—Rev. Don Southworth, executive director,
Unitarian Universalist Ministers Association

Introduction

Conscious and deliberate acts of caring are a uniquely human attribute. The need to care and to be cared for are essential to the survival of all human groups. We create communities, cultural norms, ethical frameworks, social constructs, and beliefs that help guide our choices to make our lives meaningful and understandable. We form families and care for them by nurturing their growth and development. We develop shared interests and identities with other families, seeking to sustain our well-being and survival. And in those times when we are baffled, suffering, scared, or engulfed in physical pain or moral dilemmas, we have traditionally sought care from religious institutions and spiritual understandings. To these we bring the fullness of our spirits to be acknowledged and addressed, seeking love and authentic relationships. We bring our desire for forgiveness, mercy, and autonomy. We bring our claims of faith that provide meaning amid the insecurity of life. We bring our need for hope and vision, to satisfy the self-consciousness of our finitude. We want to be ethical and honest, humble and grateful, in a world that is sometimes unjust and evil. We bring to religion and spiritual sources our broken, ill-formed questions and curiosities to be tended to, laid bare, and examined.

Most religious and spiritual traditions have well-developed caring arts that include healing, reconciling, guiding, and sustaining those in distress or crisis. Part of the work of priests, shamans, ministers, imams, rabbis, and other spiritual guides is to hold sacred and safe places for the unpredictable spiritual needs of their communities. These caregivers provide receptivity, relatedness, and focused presence; all of which invites ambiguity, transcendence, mystery, and transformation. These actions also encourage members of their communities to offer these gifts to one another.

The figure of the chaplain in the western world has always been ambiguous—a clergyperson whose duties lie away from ecclesial authority or the demands of a congregation. In secular institutions such as hospitals, prisons, and the military, the chaplain's role remains ambiguous since, unlike doctors, guards, or soldiers, the chaplain is an explicit broker between the sacred and the secular. The role of the chaplain and the social perception of chaplaincy in America have both changed significantly since World War II. In the mid-twentieth century, patients, inmates, and soldiers understood that chaplains had specific ministerial resources that were particular to each denomination, such that Catholic priests, for example, could offer services that no other denomination's chaplains could. Today, chaplains practice a "ministry of presence" with those seeking support and serve as partners for exploring issues of meaning and purpose often initiated by a crisis. Chaplains are trained to de-emphasize their individual religious identities so that they can provide a non-imposing, non-coercive presence, letting care seekers take the lead regarding how specifically religious they want to get. At its core, chaplaincy is about bringing the sacred out of the church, mosque, synagogue, and temple to offer it to the people, wherever they are in need. Chaplains meet people wherever they are, physically or spiritually, and offer support. They listen. They bring a sense of the sacred, of wonder and awe, to a secular context. They address particular needs and assist care seekers in meaning making and reflective processes during incarceration, on the Navy ship, in the treatment program, in the hospital room, and on college campuses. In all these endeavors, chaplains provide authentic human caring to the non-religious and the religious. They aim to create and hold a safe space where people can bring all of themselves and be vulnerable. Chaplains work to be available, to be present, for people to face their fears in the presence of someone with time to care.

History of Unitarian and Universalist Chaplains

Unitarian Universalist ministers have historically taken our faith far beyond the bounds of local congregations. They have brought their prophetic voices to social justice work, led community organizing efforts, and developed non-profit agencies. Yet, the history of Unitarian and Universalist chaplains who worked and work in institutional settings has never been systematically chronicled. There are no chapters in the tomes of denominational history books, or lists of famous UU chaplains on the UUA website. Our seminary libraries have little primary research material or documents that tell the stories of chaplains in our tradition.

In fact, the development of this collection of essays required a painstaking search to simply identify and locate Unitarian Universalist chaplains throughout our association. While Jewish, Catholic, Muslim, Lutheran, Methodist, and Buddhist chaplains have denominational organizations, listings, and conferences to keep their work visible, UU chaplains are generally isolated in the institutional silos of their employment.

Unitarian Universalist chaplains' concern and reverence for the dignity and worth of every human being is a foundational principle for their chaplaincy. Whether theist, deist, humanist, atheist, Christian, Jewish, Buddhist, or pagan, UU chaplains are engaged in the daily task of exploring the theological and philosophical constructs of *why and how we care*. This much-needed conversation about our theology and praxis is starting to take form as small groups of UU chaplains begin to find each other in different regions of the country. I hope that this collection of essays will support the continued development of chaplains and chaplaincy throughout our association. The voices, stories, and theological reflections in this volume can also provide guidance for caring teams in congregations or assist parish ministers seeking new spiritual intervention strategies. This collection can also serve as a discernment tool for seminarians interested in chaplaincy but uncertain of the available career paths. Finally, this book is for the people in our pews, and those on their way, who want to know, "Will someone be there for me when I need them and how will they care for me?"

The work of contemporary Unitarian Universalist chaplains continues a rich legacy of spiritual care outside the parish. While definitive research on the history of chaplaincy still needs to be taken up in another project, here are some anecdotes, events, and circumstances involving UU chaplains in our history.

Military

The first recorded notation of a chaplain from our tradition comes from the Revolutionary War. George Washington commissioned the first fifteen military chaplains in 1775 to attend to the spiritual needs of the troops. Universalist minister John Murray numbered among them, to serve in the Continental Army. Later, thirty Unitarians served as chaplains during the Civil War for the Union. Rev. Arthur B. Fuller had a deep opposition to slavery that drew him not only to chaplaincy, but later to serve as an active combatant in the Battle of Fredericksburg, where he was killed. Today there is a vibrant community of Unitarian Universalist military chaplains that is well integrated into our association. They serve in both active duty and in the reserves.

Government

Three Unitarian chaplains and one Universalist chaplain have ministered to the members of the House of Representatives and the Senate. Unitarian minister Jared Sparks was appointed chaplain of the House in 1821, followed by Unitarian William Henry Channing in 1863 and Universalist Henry Couden in 1895. In the Senate, there have been two Unitarian chaplains: Edward Everett Hale, appointed in 1903, and Ulysses Grant Baker Pierce, appointed in 1909. In 1865, when the Thirteenth Amendment to the Constitution was signed that abolished slavery, Unitarian chaplain William Henry Channing invited Henry Garner, a minister of great esteem, to deliver the sermon, which was the first time an African American had addressed a congressional body. With the outbreak of the Civil War, many wounded soldiers were coming to Washington. Channing, who was also the minister at All Souls Church, turned the building into a hospital, and he trained his congregants to be chaplains to help the wounded. Channing also served as chaplain for one of the largest hospitals in Washington, D.C., where he was the only minister who brought a liberal loving message to those devastated by war, chaos, and displacement.

Colleges and Universities

Unitarians were perhaps the first to develop a denominational initiative for campus ministry by establishing churches in college towns and thus developing an opportunity for college chaplaincy. Today, Unitarian Universalist ministers can be found on numerous campuses serving the specific needs of UU students by providing spiritual care and affirming their faith through worship and service. Their presence on campuses has often placed these chaplains and the UU students at the center of social and economic justice campaigns and controversies. UU chaplains have helped to further the spirit of ecumenism and interfaith work among religious groups as they have navigated religious pluralism in the university environment.

Prisons and Rehabilitation Centers

While Dorothea Dix was not a minister, she was a Unitarian who volunteered to teach Sunday School for women inmates of the East Cambridge Jail in Massachusetts in 1841. There she found her calling as a prison reformer. Shocked by the terrible conditions in the jail, she felt an obligation to change them for the better. This led her to undertake a systematic tour of the jails and prisons in Massachusetts. She detailed her findings in her 1843 "Memorial to the Massachusetts Legislature." Many examples of her "chaplaincy" can be found in that document that describes the terrible conditions she felt obliged to change by bringing them to the policy makers.

Charles Spear was a Universalist minister in Massachusetts in the early 1800s who asked that the state, "Spare the criminal." He declared capital punishment "an unjust and arbitrary exercise of power, an instrument not fit for the Republic." He said, "I want our prisons to be more like hospitals." Early in 1845, Spear began to edit and publish *The Prisoner's Friend*, a journal devoted to transforming the purpose of prisons from punishment to rehabilitation. As a chaplain he visited prisoners, helped many parolees, and ran a halfway house for ex-convicts. He became known as "the prisoner's friend." Following in that tradition, the Church of the Larger Fellowship serves Unitarian Universalists who are incarcerated and it provides chaplain ministry to these men and women through letters and publications.

Hospitals and Hospices

Unitarians and Universalists were among the first ministers and doctors to create the educational model of Clinical Pastoral Education (CPE), which has become the foundational training method for professional chaplains today. Richard Cabot was a Unitarian medical doctor who in 1925 called for a "clinical year" in a medical setting for theological students at Harvard Divinity School. Understanding the value of clinical supervision, and influenced by the progressive education movement of Unitarian John Dewey, Cabot provided the first framework for combining theological and clinical education, which is still required for the training of seminarians. The pastoral care and education movement organized as The Council for Clinical Training of Theological Students on January 21, 1930, in the home of Samuel Atkins Eliot, minister of Arlington Street Church in Boston. The liberal theology and interfaith orientation of hospital chaplaincy was developed by Unitarians. The majority of Unitarian Universalist chaplains today serve in hospitals and hospice settings and on ethics committees in medical centers.

First Responders and Disaster Response

Like other clergy, Unitarian Universalist ministers show up when people are hurting in public settings where an unexpected crisis event has taken place, such as a terror attack, explosion, earthquake, shooting, or infrastructure accident. While less formalized than chaplaincy in institutional settings, these ministers provide direct, immediate trauma chaplaincy care to those in distress. In 2002, the Unitarian Universalist Trauma Response Ministry (UUTRM) was founded. Since that time it has responded to more than a hundred crisis situations from natural disasters to personal tragedies within congregations. The UUTRM includes about fifty volunteers, 80 percent of them ministers, who are available to help congregations when called upon. Members of the ministry team come in on short notice to assist local clergy in providing spiritual care after disasters and other events. In addition, Unitarian Universalists have served and continue to serve as chaplains to police and fire departments throughout the country.

The Unitarian Universalist clergy in this volume represent those called to engage crisis in institutional settings. These chaplains are required to meet specific professional standards set forth by the Association of Professional Chaplains and the Association of Clinical Pastoral Education. These two organizations provide training, oversight, and accreditation for Board Certification, which is becoming increasingly required for long-term employment. Given this distinction, the essays in this volume do not reflect the work of laity and clergy who serve as Unitarian Universalist chaplains on college and university campuses.

In addition, members of the UUTRM, who show up to respond to trauma in public settings, provide many of the same interventions that chaplains provide, yet they do not consider themselves chaplains by definition; therefore their work is not included in this volume either.

Trends in Unitarian Universalist Ministry

The majority of the 1,004 Unitarian Universalist ministers are based in and serve our 1,038 congregations. Community ministers serve in administrative positions within the association, serve in the non-profit sector, or work as spiritual entrepreneurs and chaplains. Recently, a trend has been emerging. Many seminarians entering the ministry realize that they may need to consider a bi-vocational path to ministry, as fewer opportunities for full-time ministry are available. Some seminaries and divinity schools that train UU ministers are developing master of divinity programs that focus on chaplaincy. These schools are partnering with chaplaincy training centers to develop resources and new opportunities for professional development, thus expanding the exposure and base of potential UU chaplains and clinical educators.

According to the Unitarian Universalist Ministers Association, in 2013, 27 percent of ministers were working as community ministers outside of congregations, the majority of them working as chaplains in large secular institutions. Like their historical predecessors, they infuse the theologies and beliefs of Unitarian Universalism into the profession of chaplaincy. In fact, UU chaplains are seen as very desirable to these institutions because they bring a broad, reasoned, inclusive, and fluid approach to chaplaincy. As the adult population continues to trend toward having fewer bonds to traditional institutional religion, as they explore more broad-based spiritual expressions, Unitarian Universalist chaplains will continue to be instrumental in shaping spiritual care in the future.

Inherent Worth and Dignity

JANE ELLEN MAULDIN

It's 7:30 in the morning when I enter the front doors of the busy urban hospital that I serve in New Orleans, Louisiana. The halls downstairs are quiet at this early hour. I pass the gift shop, still dark and locked. A nurse trudges past me on her way out the door after her twelve-hour shift. She manages a smile at my cheery "Good morning!" A maintenance guy carries a tool box, already on his way to fix some essential part of this huge complex of buildings. He grins a "Hey how ya doin'?" to my greeting.

I am alone on the elevator, but when I step out onto the third floor to go to my office, I see family members heading toward the surgery waiting room. Already, down long hallways and through many sets of double doors, surgeons, nurses, and anesthesiologists are hard at work with mothers and fathers, sons and daughters, while family members pace and worry, gratefully accepting hot coffee from the early-morning volunteers.

This hospital is a place of hope and fear. This is a place of death and life. It's a place where boundaries touch and overlap. Seeming miracles take place in the cardiology lab. Unexpected death brings dismay in the labor and delivery suite. It's a place where nothing is sure and everything matters.

My job is to be present. I am here to listen to, walk with, hold hands with, cry, laugh, and pray with those who are living the excruciating joy and sorrow that exist here on the boundary, here at the intersection of death and life. So often, there is

nothing for me to say. So often, the job, the challenge, is simply
to be present, to be a witness and a companion on the boundary.
I am a hospital chaplain. On most days, I visit dozens of
patients and their family members, and have conversations with
many nurses, doctors, aides, housekeepers, and therapists who
work with them. Who will I see today? When I get to my office,
I print out the patient list and highlight the names of all the
new patients. Likely, today I will see many of them, young and
old, men and women. They may be Caucasian, African American, Asian, or Hispanic; Christian, Jewish, agnostic, Buddhist,
Muslim, or Unitarian Universalist. Rich or poor. Some are completely alone and some are surrounded by loving family. All are
living on the boundary. Is it cancer? A sinus infection? Is it my
heart? Can they fix it one more time? Hope and fear. . . .

I take the elevator to a medical/surgical unit and enter an
older woman's room. Let's call her Mrs. James. My patient list
reports that she is eighty-seven years old. Religion unknown.
"Come on in!" invites the woman sitting beside her. "I am her
daughter, Gloria. This is her granddaughter, Rebecca." She indicates a tall young woman standing beside the bed. I shake hands
all around and introduce myself. "I'm Chaplain Jane. I'm a chaplain here at the hospital, and I like to meet our new patients."
I turn to the elderly lady in the bed. "How are you doing, Mrs.
James?" She reaches for me and I take her hand. "Who . . . who
. . . ?" "THIS IS THE CHAPLAIN, MOM!" yells Gloria. "Oh!"
says Mrs. James. (Turns out Mrs. James is a bit hard of hearing.) "Well, hello!" She welcomes me into the family and tells
me about the children, and the grandchildren, and the great-
grandchildren. No great-great-grandchildren, yet! I learn about
difficult times back in Mississippi, about an absent husband and
raising nine children, none of them gone to jail or doing drugs.
All of them good children. And I learn about love, forgiveness,
and the tremendous power of family, the power of community. I
learn about the power of faith in good times and in bad.

Eventually, I offer, "Mrs. James, would you like us to pray
together, while I'm here?" "What?" "PRAY. WOULD YOU LIKE
US TO PRAY TOGETHER?" "Oh, yes!" (This is a woman who
has lived her eighty-seven years with gusto!) So Mrs. James,

Gloria, Rebecca, and I take hands. And we pray. I start out (basically yelling), "Dear God, precious God, who is always with us, in good times and in bad, on the mountaintop and in the valley . . ." But soon we are all taking turns: praising and thanking, and speaking of pain and trouble, and asking blessings of healing in body and spirit, and praising and thanking again. The prayer rises and falls in our little circle, and eventually we come to "Amen. Thank you, Jesus. Thank you. Amen." A quiet. A beauty of sharing. Mystery.

As a Unitarian Universalist, I claim a theology that recognizes that truth flows from numerous sources and that various religious paths can lead us toward a life of love and service. I believe that we are born and live as part of that creative, universal wholeness that is ultimately unnamable yet that many call by the name God. Because of circumstances that wound us or bad choices that we make, we often become blind to, or alienated from, the reality that the Holy is all around us and within us, sustaining and supporting us. My theology of spiritual care calls me to attempt to live daily with awareness of this holy reality.

If there is God, if there is holiness and mystery, surely it was and is there, with Mrs. James and her family. Now, it's pretty clear to me that Mrs. James thinks of God in different images, with different stories and metaphors, than I do, but something happened in that prayer. Something amazing. But what was it? Was it God?

As a chaplain, I work in close proximity to many people, in small rooms, sharing usually quiet conversations. However, when I leave the hospital at night and look up at the stars, I become aware once again that we live at the intersection of two infinities. A walk on a clear moonless night reveals a universe of billions of stars—a universe, we are told, that is endlessly expanding. It is as if our galaxies are dots on a balloon which is being blown out and out and out. There is no end, no limit to its expansion. I can't imagine it. It is infinite space, infinite time. Infinity.

On the other hand, molecular physicists confront us with yet another startling assertion: the infinity of the small. You can observe this infinity any moment you choose. Look at your hand: There before you are cells, molecules, atoms, protons, neutrons, and electrons . . . and even smaller subatomic particles with peculiar names such as *quarks* and *Higgs bosons*. The smaller the particles, the less distinct from other particles they become, until all is finally the same stuff, which is, in essence, energy. Not only that, but we will never fully observe these particles. This assertion is called the uncertainty principle. If we can accurately observe the position of a particle, we cannot know its momentum or its movement at the same time.

When I first walked into a Unitarian Universalist church, some thirty-five years ago, I did so having rejected the loving yet manipulative Father God of my childhood. I could no longer fit what I was learning about the infinities of space and the infinities of molecular biology into the tight theological pigeonholes demanded by my mainline Protestant upbringing. However, I still had the sense that, beyond all definitions and doctrines, something infinite and good existed in which I participated. What was it? Could I ever begin to understand it or name it? As a chaplain today, I continue to develop these questions: How can I speak of an ultimately indefinable "God" with patients and families? How can I use language to describe that which is indescribable?

The Unitarian theologian Henry Nelson Wieman asked similar questions in his *The Source of Human Good*, and some of his answers have helped to guide my pastoral practice. At a time when humanism and theism were at odds in our American theological schools, Wieman argued for a third way, a middle path. He proclaimed that "God is an object of sensuous experience," that God is "as real as a toothache." However, rather than relying on history or doctrine, Wieman argued that we can only understand the nature of God by paying attention to our own life experiences, guided by reason. His own experience and reason led Wieman to conclude that God is that power which is the integrative activity at the heart of all reality. He called this activity "creative interchange." Our commitment and our devotion, Wieman declared, must be to the creative good that is the activity of God. Thus we experience holiness, God (or whatever name we call it), when we participate in the process of creative interchange. For Wieman, *God* is a verb.

I appreciate Wieman all the more when I remember what the voice of God is said to have declared to Moses from the burning bush. The translators of the King James Bible rendered the Hebrew words emanating from that bush as "I Am That I Am." However, Rabbi Arthur Waskow argues in "Do We Need to ReName God?" that this is a mistranslation, that a more accurate translation is "I Will Be Who I Will Be." What Moses needed in order to awaken the Israelites to claim their freedom was a name of God that says the universe is becoming and that reality can change. What we need in order to imagine possibilities and freedom from present suffering is a sense of holiness that moves with us in that process. The twentieth-century process theologian Alfred North Whitehead similarly recognized that all of reality is movement, is becoming.

So what happened when Mrs. James, Gloria, Rebecca, and I held hands and prayed together? It's highly unlikely that Mrs. James, whose aging body is very sick, will experience a "healing" of her physical ailments. However, as we prayed together, there was a different kind of healing in her room, a renewal of hope, of love, and of faith in connection to something real and eternal. Mrs. James and her family use traditional Christian language to describe their relationship with God and Jesus. As a chaplain, when I pray with a Baptist, a Jew, a Muslim, or a Unitarian Universalist, I pray with the understanding that, whatever language or metaphors we use, our shared prayer is a shared experience of the Holy.

Leaving Mrs. James's room, I climb the stairs up two flights to the head injury rehabilitation unit. There is a new young man there. I wonder: What is his story? Is he able to speak? Or will my ministry to him be with eyes, a smile, and a few words spoken with care? Will I hold his hand, and will he feel it if I do? Will he nod "yes" if I ask him if he would like me to offer a prayer? And if he does, what prayer should I say? What prayer can I offer a young man who sustained such a terrible brain injury—let's say in a car wreck; it often is—that he might never walk, or speak, again? How do I offer a presence of hope to a young man who may feel bereft of all hope?

Usually, before I enter a patient's room, I stand outside the door and take a slow, deep breath, centering myself to be fully present. I come into each patient's room grounded in my commitment to the first Unitarian Universalist Principle, which is to "affirm and promote the inherent worth and dignity of every person." My commitment to that principle has its roots in several sources, especially in a Jewish teaching that we each carry a spark of the divine and become most fully human and most able to experience God or holiness within human relationships. In particular, Martin Buber, a Jewish theologian of the last century, described two ways of being in relationship: "I-It" and "I-Thou." He wrote, "One becomes human only in I-Thou relationships, for only these call a person into unique wholeness. . . . As I become I, I say Thou." Even so, he wrote, God is the "eternal Thou."

On the other hand, Buber suggests that when we are in an "I-It" relationship with another entity, we experience it as separate from ourselves, something that we analyze, categorize, and study, as we might study a tree. Thus, in chaplaincy, we may hear a patient describe a fact or make a statement, such as "My mother died when I was young" or "Religion doesn't do much for me anymore," but this statement seems separate from us. We are not in relationship with that truth, with the other person, or with the Eternal until we move deeper and relate to the other person in the sacredness of the "I-Thou" relationship. I have felt that "I-Thou" relationship with the family of a dying woman when, at my invitation, four individuals came from their separate lonely corners of the room to form a sacred circle around their mother, to touch her and tell her that they loved her as she took her last breaths. I have felt that "I-Thou" relationship with the Catholic priest with whom I share chaplaincy as we co-officiated at a memorial service for a beloved staff nurse. We led nurses, aides, and physicians in prayer, song, expressions of grief, and the beginnings of healing as we encouraged each other, cried, and laughed together with our beloved hospital congregation.

This relationship is often not easy. It is risky to join another person as they step into the valley and open themselves to the pain, confusion, and grief that they encounter there. I have heard an inexperienced chaplain describe how he attempted to comfort an anxious patient by saying, "God will take care of it" and "It will be all right." My experience is that when I offer such platitudes, I am usually standing apart from the other person, in an "I-It" relationship. I am not recognizing and honoring the inherent worth and dignity of the other person. I have not stepped down from a distant position to join them in an "I-Thou" relationship.

Thus, I understand my pastoral role to be to walk with, listen to, and relate one-on-one with people who are hurting, confused, grieving, or at a change-point in their lives. Rabbi Harold Kushner writes, "Several years ago I read of an experiment conducted by the University of Wisconsin's Center for the Study of Pain. A number of volunteers were tested to see how long they could keep a bare foot in a bucket of ice water. One of the things they learned was that if there was someone else in the room, they could keep their foot in the bucket twice as long. The presence of another caring person doubles the amount of pain a person can endure. That is what God does when God sends us people to be with us in our grief." Theologian Dorothy Soelle similarly reflected that being alone, without human companionship, is an essential ingredient of the deepest levels of human suffering. Simply put, my pastoral role in the presence of suffering is to be a caring person. Even more, it is to be a connector, a witness, a reminder that the suffering person is not alone, either in this reality or in the greater reality of all existence. My work begins with the hope that I may offer a non-anxious presence that is grounded in the "eternal Thou."

So I climb the stairs to the head injury rehabilitation unit. I take a deep breath, knock on the young man's door, and go in. Matt is sitting strapped into a wheelchair. I introduce myself, and he greets me with his eyes and a clumsy nod of his head. I ask his permission to pull up a chair to be near him, and offer a few words, acknowledging his struggles and his challenges in the days ahead, and thanking him for the privilege of being with him as he works to get stronger. Eventually, I ask if he would like us to pray together. Matt nods "yes" and lifts his hand slightly. I take it in mine and close my eyes, but I sense that he is watching me. I pause and breathe, and then I pray. I pray for the presence of holiness here. I pray that Matt will feel a sense of eternal love, in good times and in bad, in sickness and in health. I pray for a blessing of healing, in body and in spirit. Does prayer work? Who knows? Some scientific double-blind studies seem to indicate that prayer, somehow, sometimes, makes a difference. I certainly do not believe that prayer sparks an intervention by a conscious God who, on a whim and because I asked, is actually going to change his mind about who should be sick and who shouldn't. But is prayer a focusing of energy from out there, in the cosmos? Is it a deep welling-up of healing power from within the person who knows he or she is being prayed for? Is it Wieman's creative event that occurs when Matt and I pray together? Is it an experience of Buber's "I-Thou" relationship? Is it all of these, or something more? I just don't know. But this I do know: When I finish the prayer with Matt and open my eyes, he is looking at me. He is gripping my hand. And when our eyes meet, he breathes a deep sigh, and nods, "Yes."

My theology of pastoral practice, therefore, is that when I go into a patient's room, I do more than simply "visit the sick." I go there hoping to offer an "I-Thou" relationship that may be helpful for their physical or spiritual healing. However, our relationship and the terms of the pastoral encounter are grounded in the other person's willingness to grant me authority to be their chaplain. I walk into Matt's room wearing the trappings of hospital authority: a name tag that says *Chaplain*. I also enter with a sense of internal authority, the knowledge that I have skills and experience that some people find useful as they struggle with grief, loss, life changes, and ethical decision making. However, the authority that really matters when I walk into Matt's room is whatever authority he grants me as his chaplain. Rev. Sam Southard explains in *Comprehensive Pastoral Care* that in pastoral conversations, the person in authority (the chaplain) moves toward the other person out of care and concern. The other person (the patient) feels that and then authorizes the first to be their chaplain. The authority is relational.

For many years in congregational ministry, I felt my pastoral authority to be largely rooted in my mastery of content and ideas and confirmed by my competent functioning, the way I offered leadership in worship and pastoral support to individuals and groups. As a chaplain, however, I recognize that my pastoral authority flows from a different source, a way of being: from who I am as pastor and person. I now claim my pastoral authority as an ongoing holistic integration of skills, experience, insight, and relationships rather than as a by-product of diplomas on the wall. That pastoral authority is activated daily by those who authorize me to be their chaplain. So when Matt welcomes me into his room with a gaze and a nod, and when he reaches out his hand . . . that is when I become his chaplain.

It is a humbling experience and an amazing privilege to be invited into the rooms and lives of men and women who do not know me, yet nevertheless welcome me to join them and hear their joys and sorrows. I go into their rooms to be with them, to listen, and—if they invite me—to be with them in an "I-Thou" relationship. It is by their invitation that my pastoral care occurs on different levels. Wayne Oates describes pastoral care as consisting of five levels of ever-deepening involvement with people: friendship, comfort, confession, teaching, and counseling. Oates writes that the majority of pastoral care conversations occur on the levels of friendship and comfort. Even here, if I am fully present and respectful, I have experienced "I-Thou" relationships, as I did with Matt. More frequently, however, I experience an "I-Thou" relationship with a patient, family member, or staff member when they grant me authority as their chaplain to join them on a deeper level of confession, teaching, or counseling.

For example, when I go into Ms. Samuels's room later in the morning, she tells me that she is worried about some tests that she has just undergone. She moves our pastoral conversation to the deeper level of confession, as she describes feeling guilty about her fear and explores how she might grow a renewed trust in God. After some conversation, she says, "It's in the Lord's hands." I ask her if she would like me to offer a prayer with her. "Yes," she says, "I want to ask the Lord for strength. And that it's not cancer." She reaches out her hand to me. I hold her hand in mine and we close our eyes. At that moment, her oncologist, Dr. Marks, walks briskly into the room. "Oh, I'll come back in a minute," he says, and does a U-turn toward the door. "Oh, no, please join us," I urge, and reach out my other hand toward him. Dr. Marks comes back into the room and the three of us hold hands in a circle. I offer a prayer using Ms. Samuels's theological language, thanking God for the gift of life, asking for God's wisdom and guidance for Dr. Marks and for all of the doctors and nurses at our hospital, praying that it not be cancer that Ms. Samuels is facing, but that whatever may come, she may know God's love for her, now and always. When I conclude the prayer and we all open our eyes, there is a moment of calm, of peace, that was not among us before. By participating in prayer together, we experience the "Thou" in one another, and the sacredness of each of us being in relationship with the "Thou," together. When I stop back by Ms. Samuels's room approximately fifteen minutes later I am surprised to see that Dr. Marks is still sitting at the end of her bed, talking with her. I silently wonder if their shared prayer has influenced the length of his conversation with her.

Something happened there. Wieman might call it "creative interchange." Buber might call it an experience of an "I-Thou" relationship. The Jewish mystic Abraham Joshua Heschel called it awe in his book *Who Is Man?*: "Awe is an intuition for the dignity of all things, a realization that things not only are what they are but also stand, however remotely, for something supreme. Awe is a sense for the transcendence, for the reference everywhere to mystery beyond all things." Surely at Ms. Samuels's bedside that morning, for just a moment, an analysis of her medical condition took second place to the sense that we all had of the presence of the eternal. Together, Ms. Samuels, Dr. Marks, and I experienced awe, the sacred "Thou" amongst us.

As a hospital chaplain, I must not only step into the boundary land and risk being in "I-Thou" relationship with people who are experiencing deep suffering, but also walk alongside other hospital staff who are taking that same courageous step. Daily, I witness nurses, patient care techs, physicians, and therapists offering not only medical treatment but also deep levels of human companionship to patients and families in distress. Offering this companionship is sometimes spiritually and physically exhausting for hospital staff. As I pass down the hallway of the oncology unit at midday, a nurse named Rachel answers my greeting with a deep sigh and a shake of her head. I follow her into the staff break room where she will quickly eat her lunch, and learn from her that today she is caring for Marie, a young woman in her twenties who has been fighting cancer for almost a year. The cancer has metastasized, and Marie is nearing the end of her life. The nurse is frustrated at Marie's parents, who insist that "everything should be done." "Why don't they just let her be?" Rachel demands. "She's an adult. She says she's tired. Just tired. I don't want to keep prodding and poking her, when it's not going to do any good!" I hear her frustration. "That must be so hard, to have to keep hurting her, when you feel it's not going to help her." She looks at me sadly. "Rachel, how are you letting Marie know you care about her?" I learn that Rachel tries to be very gentle with Marie, talks to her softly, wipes her face, and lets her know frequently, in many ways, how much she is cared for. "And do you think she gets the message?" I ask. "Oh yes. Sometimes she sort of smiles. It's really hard for her, but she knows I care for her." "Hmmmm," I muse. "You know, Rachel, the way I see it is that God is love." Rachel nods. "And when you care for her, you are doing God's work. You wish you could change her life, her parents, her illness . . . " I pause. She chews her sandwich. "And you can't. But I believe you are doing holy work, loving her, despite her pain, her crazy parents, everything. She is surrounded by love, in her last days. That is really holy work. . . . At least, that's how I see it as your chaplain." Rachel breathes a deep sigh. She smiles slightly. She stands up and throws away her juice bottle. "I hope so. I do hope so. Thank you!" She hugs me and heads back out to her patients.

Rachel is trained to be a healer of bodies. However, Marie's situation has relegated her to a place where, by her estimation, her physical care mostly just causes further suffering. My relationship with Rachel as her chaplain over several years has led her to trust that if she describes her fear and spiritual pain, I will honor her struggle and will accompany her as she finds her way. I hope that my pastoral care with Rachel also helps empower her to be with Marie in deeper and more profound ways, so that this patient and this nurse may experience a transformative "I-Thou" relationship as they journey together in the boundary land between life and death. That boundary land is a strange and foreign place for so many of us. Yet that is where I have experienced meaning and hope with patients and staff, time and again.

After a very full morning on our medical/surgical, rehabilitation, and oncology units, I am paged to come quickly to provide pastoral support to a family whose loved one, Mr. Jonas, is dying in our intensive care unit after years of illness. Together, several of his sisters, brothers, and friends stand vigil and pray around his bed. More family arrive, including a deacon from their small, rural Louisiana church. Eventually, the deacon moves to the head of Mr. Jonas's bed and starts singing. The singing is low, slow, and powerful—prayer in song. Two brothers join in, carrying harmony. They sing songs that I do not know, but some phrases are familiar: "If you get there before I do" and "He's comin' home." The normal hubbub of the busy ICU quiets. The glass door to Mr. Jonas's room is open, with only a curtain separating us from the other people in the unit. The power of the music reaches out to many others: nurses, doctors, and other patients. I stand with the family around the bed, swaying and humming, praying with them in song. I feel that I am moving between two worlds, the world of faith and the world of the hospital medical routine. I also feel fully, authentically present in both worlds. Mr. Jonas's family embrace me and ask me to lead a prayer. The hospital personnel seem to relax, able to step out of the room and trust what is happening, because I am there. As Mr. Jonas takes his last breaths, I ask the deacon to lead us in singing again, to "sing him on home." There is truly eternal peace in that room, and we all know it.

As I leave the ICU, reflecting on what has just happened, I feel deeply humbled to have been included in that sacred, powerful family faith event. Everyone around that bedside—and everyone in the ICU—knew that something very special and very holy was happening there. There was nothing that I had to teach. My job, as their chaplain, was to be present, to be with them on the boundary between sacred and secular, between life and death; to help create a setting of safety and trust so that the family could pray and the hospital staff could do their work of helping Mr. Jonas die gently and pain-free. The "I-Thou" relationships between the family members, the deacon, other staff, and me dissolved boundaries as we stepped into a strange land beyond usual definitions and descriptions during our time together. No, we did not stop being who we each were, yet in that event I believe we all experienced something more than our individual selves.

And Mr. Jonas . . . what about him? What happens at death? There are so many possibilities, well beyond the scope of this essay, yet through my years of chaplaincy I have learned this: The greatest calm and courage I have had the privilege to witness are exhibited by those who trust that when they are in that boundary land and there is no going back to the known and familiar, the infinities of existence—the eternal "Thou," whatever we do or don't call it—do not cease when our bodies cease breathing. This courage and faith are not the exclusive property of Christians, Jews, Muslims, Unitarian Universalists, Buddhists, humanists, or any other group. My experience is that those who trust that there is meaning in the infinities, and who recognize a connection, an eternal, in which we all participate, are usually the same people who travel the boundary land with less anxiety and more peace for themselves and their families.

As my workday draws to a close, I see a last few patients, then return to my office, turn off the computer, and head down the hall toward the exit doors. It has been an exhilarating and exhausting day in an amazing hospital community of people deeply committed to relieving suffering and promoting healing, and I am aware of the tiredness in my body. A wise teacher once suggested to me that when I return home in the evening I "wash" my body and spirit clean of the suffering that I have seen. One chaplain colleague prefers long hot baths. Tonight, I will likely "wash" myself with some smudging incense and open myself to peace and healing through that ritual. I also plan to take a cup of herbal tea into my backyard, to watch the evening light fade from silver blue to soft gray and then black. The turning of the natural light helps me to turn the prayers and needs of the many people I have been with over to the Eternal Thou and to turn my own energy to my home and family.

With that plan for self-care in mind, I leave the hospital, saying a silent prayer for the nurses, doctors, technicians, and housekeepers I have seen this day. As I do, I remember several years ago when the hospital was on lockdown for Hurricane Gustav. I and hundreds of other hospital staff, and nearly one hundred patients, lived inside the hospital walls for four long days and nights as Gustav approached our coast and then made landfall with hundred-mile-an-hour winds. During the first night of lockdown, the power went out throughout the city and the hospital relied on generators to provide electricity to essential areas. Many of the staff members and patients had lost their homes in the flood following Hurricane Katrina several years previously, and many had borne significant physical, emotional, and spiritual loss and suffering following that storm. This new hurricane, Gustav, often dredged up terrible memories.

In response, Father Daniel, my priest colleague, and I offered prayer services for the hospital community following supper each evening during lockdown. With dozens of hospital staff, we sang, read psalms, prayed, and spoke from our hearts of the fear and faith that we shared. The first two evening gatherings were in the sweltering cafeteria dining hall. The second two, after the worst of the storm had passed, were held outside, as we stood in a large circle, protected from the rain by a large overhang over the entrance to the emergency room. We were a circle of men and women; Caucasian, African American, Hispanic, and Asian American; nurses, aides, cooks, therapists, secretaries, housekeepers, vice-presidents, and the CEO. We held hands, speaking loudly above the roar of the emergency generators and the startlingly loud cicadas in the tree across the street. I started the prayer, Father Daniel offered his gentle Christian words, and then one person after another spoke aloud their gratitude, hope, sorrow, and relief. I concluded the service with a final, inclusive prayer and benediction. These hospital staff had watched their family members leave town without them, staying to care for patients and face a potentially deadly storm together. I was humbled by their generosity of body and spirit, despite their own woundedness following Hurricane Katrina. Every evening following the services, individuals sought me out for spiritual and emotional support. On the second night, Luke, a social worker, wondered aloud with me "what the heck" God had to do with all this. "Hmmm," I said. "There are many answers to that question. I'm curious what you think about that." "I don't know," he said. "Well, why don't you take a look around you, pray about it through the day tomorrow, and then let's talk again," I said. The next evening, we found one another on the ambulance ramp. The storm had passed, missing New Orleans, and anxiety levels were markedly lower. "Well, Luke, what do you think God has to do with all this?" I asked. "Well, I sure don't think he brings the hurricane. But there's been a lot of love and care around here, this week," he mused. "So . . . ?" I asked. "Guess I'm rooted in that 'God is love' thing," he chuckled.

My job that day and every day is to live in the boundary world, that in-between place which is often immensely frightening. Will this storm destroy everything I know and love, again . . . or simply knock down a few trees and electric poles? Is my illness a recurrence of cancer . . . or just a cold? Nothing is sure here. Just as the infinity of subatomic particles cannot be measured, and the infinity of space is beyond our (current) understanding, so also the infinity of meaning cannot be measured in this boundary world between life and death, hopelessness and hope, where I walk with the people I serve. The sacredness of the moment exists on this boundary edge that doesn't hold still, that is no place and many places at once. It is, rather, not a place but an event, so its truth cannot be accurately described with words. It is most fully understood experientially. It is acknowledged in the sigh, in the relaxing of shoulders, in the tears finally flowing freely. I am a chaplain when another person invites me to step into the deep boundary water with them, trusting from within our "I-Thou" relationship that I am unafraid of this place and will not leave them alone there, and that perhaps, as we travel together, infinities will meet, healing will begin, holiness will occur, and love will be real.

Head, Heart, and Holy Ground

KATHY RIEGELMAN

The day was like many others in the hospital—making rounds to the nursing units, routine visits, seeing patients whose referral to me had appeared on my printer, responding to emergent needs. The day had been reasonably paced, which is unusual for the weekend, when we have only one chaplain in house. I'd had time to make a list of the referrals and see most of them. One referral stated that the patient's family requested a chaplain's visit. I knocked on the patient's door, introduced myself, and found that she was not very awake or alert. She did, however, respond positively to my visit and offer of prayer. We had a brief visit and prayed together, and I left a note for her family letting them know I had been to see her.

About a week later I walked by this same patient's room and noticed she had guests. I introduced myself and was delighted to see that she was more awake and able to interact with her visitors. They turned out to be her pastor and his wife. The pastor was an African-American Pentecostal, and he and I "clicked." We had a lively discussion about the state of the world, ministry, and the importance of reaching out to our youth through teaching and example, rather than by being "preachy." The patient and the pastor's wife both took in our conversation and talked quietly with each other. The general mood in the room was upbeat and positive. The patient seemed to be enjoying our interaction. She seemed glad this conversation was taking place in her presence.

As the conversation wound down, I turned to the patient, wanting to give her my full attention before the visit ended. She looked me straight in the eye and said something I did not understand. The pastor repeated the few words the patient had spoken, and then the patient continued. Still, I couldn't understand a word. And then I got it—she was speaking in tongues. The patient continued, the words that I did not understand flowing from her effortlessly. When she finished, the pastor continued, also speaking in tongues. When he finished, there was no doubt in my mind or heart what had taken place. The patient and her pastor had blessed both my ministry and me. I returned their blessing, praying for the patient's health and her pastor's ministry. We said our goodbyes and I left the room, feeling very blessed, very full, very peaceful, present, and centered, and very amazed.

Reflecting on this experience led me to recall a story Diana Eck shared in her book *Encountering God: A Spiritual Journey from Bozeman to Banaras.* Eck describes her visit to a temple in southern India. In this vast and beautiful temple resides a huge image of Vishnu, reclining on a serpent that represents eternity. Eck entered the temple along with a crowd of Hindu pilgrims and moved through the circular corridors to its center. It was evening and time for *arati,* the evening offering of oil lamps. As the drums and bells began, the attendants flung open the doors of the inner sanctum where the image of the reclining Vishnu resided. As they honored Vishnu with the waving of many small lamps, the worshippers strained to see the image in the semidarkness and press of the crowd. No one could see the whole of Vishnu from any one of the many doorways where they stood. At the end of the ritual, the last lamp was brought out and offered as a blessing to the people. Eck, along with several hundred Hindu women, reached out to receive the blessing. She touched the lamp, then touched her forehead with the blessing.

Eck recognized that her experience as a Christian had to be different from that of the Hindus. "But we shared the sense of delight and revelation as the doors were opened," she writes, "and perhaps some sense of both the majesty and mystery of the Divine. I thought of nothing at the time. It was a moment of total presence, not of reflection." Eck's faith as a Christian deepened as she attempted to take in the whole of the image of Vishnu, which she could not do from any one vantage point. She felt challenged to a deeper place of faith as she came to understand that the God she believes in as a Christian is also too vast to be understood from any one perspective. She quotes A. G. Hogg as saying that "in the presence of such faith we should feel not merely respect, but religious reverence." Eck adds, "In the presence of true faith, whether Hindu or Muslim or Buddhist, we should take off our shoes, for the ground on which we are standing is holy ground. It is holy not only because it is sacred for the Hindu, Muslim, or Buddhist. It is holy ground where we ourselves may be challenged to a deeper faith."

Holy ground is the place where our faith is deepened through being "touched, challenged, or changed," as Eck describes it. Like Eck, I experienced standing on holy ground when I received a blessing in tongues because I was challenged to a deeper understanding of my faith. It was not a moment of thinking and analyzing what was happening. It was a moment of total presence when my own internal pendulum swung toward my heart.

If I had been relying on my head, my experience of the encounter with the Pentecostal and her pastor would have gone something like this: "Hm . . . according to the holiness tradition that informs Pentecostal theology, this patient is being filled with the Holy Spirit, which is talking through her in a language I cannot understand. People of this tradition call this 'speaking in tongues,' because it is referred to in the Acts of the Apostles: 'And they were all filled with the Holy Ghost, and began to speak with other tongues, as the Spirit gave them utterance.' But my faith distanced itself from highly emotive religious practices centuries ago. So this is totally not making sense and besides, it means nothing to me." My head might have further instructed me to stand politely until the patient and pastor were finished, say goodbye, and then get out of the room as quickly as possible. I am very thankful that my head did not take over in that moment, or I would have missed the profound connection. I would have missed the blessing.

Fortunately, my heart prevailed. Without me knowing what was coming, someone very different from me invited me to step out of my comfort zone. Long after Pentecostalism and Unitarian Universalism had parted ways, they had a chance meeting in a hospital room. Without losing our particularities, we were able to be there together: black and white, women and man, old and not-so-old, hospitalized and healthy, Pentecostal and Unitarian Universalist. The theological chasm between the highly emotive nature of Pentecostalism and the more restrained, rational style of Unitarian Universalism did not matter. Receiving this blessing challenged me to a deeper place in my Unitarian Universalist faith. I now understand that my faith, like that of the Pentecostals, is based in experience and emotion. While the experience that informs my faith and my chaplaincy is quieter and more internal than the ecstatic experience that informs Pentecostalism, I stood on holy ground as I learned that we share the common bond of faith that emanates from the heart.

In his essay "The Broken-Open Heart: Living with Faith and Hope in the Tragic Gap," Parker Palmer clearly describes the meaning of *heart*. He explains that it is "not merely the seat of the emotions but the core of our sense of self." Palmer's description means that experiences of holy ground are not merely emotional. That would be far too simplistic. Experiences of holy ground touch the very core of who we are. They imprint themselves on the heart, a place much deeper than words or rational explanation, a place where we can be, as Eck suggests, touched, challenged, or changed.

Unitarian Universalism recognizes the importance of heart by naming experience as essential to our faith. The first of the beautifully constructed Sources of our faith reads: "Direct experience of that transcending mystery and wonder, affirmed in all cultures, which moves us to renewal of the spirit and an openness to the forces which create and uphold life." However, our liberal religious tradition has not always considered experience, particularly personal religious experience, as the primary source of authority. The evolution of Unitarian Universalism has been marked by a tug of war between the authority of reason and rationality (the head) and that of experience and emotion (the heart).

Our eighteenth-century Unitarian forebears faced the challenge of the Great Awakening, a revivalist movement that swept through New England in the 1740s. This evangelical movement helped define American Unitarianism because it created a division between the conservatives, who believed that the revival was the work of God to restore Calvinist doctrine, and the liberals, who focused their religion more on rationality and reason. The highly emotional nature of revivalist worship was disdained by many of the liberal clergy. In his *Unitarian Universalism: A Narrative History*, David Bumbaugh describes this division as between those who "saw only madness and raw emotion and [those] who preferred a religion of reason and sobriety."

This early part of our history helps me understand the ongoing swing of the pendulum between the rationality and intellect of the head and the experience and emotion of the heart. This swing isn't seen only in our religious history and institutions. The push and pull between head and heart is also present on a personal level. As a chaplain, I also feel this internal struggle. I rely on my reason and rationality to provide a base of knowledge that informs my chaplaincy and helps keep me grounded in the often confusing world of health care. And I rely on my heart to connect with those I serve and myself.

My experience with the Pentecostal patient and her pastor opened my heart. Clarifying the source of my faith confirmed and validated that my call to ministry was a call to my heart, a call to the core of my sense of self. I am called to recognize that the sacred exists in the resilience of the human spirit and in the healing power of human relationships. And as a chaplain I am called to witness, validate, and bless this resilience, which often emerges in life's most difficult times. Being a chaplain means accepting that I cannot "fix" these difficult situations. I am not here to provide easy answers or take away the pain. Chaplaincy is about being present with those who are struggling with the spiritual and existential questions that accompany vulnerability. In other words, chaplaincy is about helping those I serve move to their hearts, to that deep place of emotion and sense of self.

The hospital environment is not particularly conducive to connecting with one's heart. The austerity of the clinical environment and the focus on medical issues can create a dualist split between body and spirit. Patients often feel disconnected from human warmth because of the focus on data, tests, diagnoses, and treatments. Patients who are "frequent flyers," who are repeatedly admitted because they suffer from chronic conditions, especially need to be recognized and treated as human beings.

Karen was one of those patients. I liked her the instant I met her. She had a determined spirit and a dry sense of humor. She had several major chronic health problems and received treatment at our hospital for about ten years. Over the years she was frequently admitted to the intensive care unit, and there were several times when we were sure she would die. As Karen and I talked about one of those close brushes with death, she told me she had seen heaven. I remember her smiling and saying that in heaven there were "lots of flowers." Karen's hospitalizations became more frequent and lengthier as the years went by. The staff kept suggesting hospice care, but she continued to resist. She wanted to live. She wanted to have more time with her family, especially her grandchildren and her significant other.

Karen came in one spring morning, and she was very sick. Although she insisted she wanted to continue aggressive care, it became evident that everything possible had already been done. She was dying. The nurse and I sat with her and talked about the difficult reality of her situation. She finally, and rather reluctantly, made her own decision that it was time for hospice. She was tired—of both the disease process and the treatments. She was tired of being poked with needles, of not having any energy, of not being able to eat what she wanted, of being confined to a wheelchair, and especially of spending so much time in the hospital.

Karen spoke from her heart about her one regret—that she and her significant other, Bill, had never been able to marry. Karen's disability payments were an important source of the family's income. If she and Bill had gotten married, she would have lost these benefits. And now it was impossible for them to get a marriage license, because Karen was too sick to leave the hospital. Karen and Bill seemed defeated. We talked about the options, and I suggested we have a wedding, marriage license or not. We agreed that being married in the eyes of God was far more important than being married in the eyes of the law.

That afternoon the hospital staff gathered in Karen's room to witness their marriage. Karen's love of flowers was well known, and one of her daughters brought a huge bouquet of brightly colored daisies from the hospital gift shop. Karen was too tired to get out of bed, and her eyes were closed throughout most of the ceremony. Bill sat next to her and held her in his arms. I affirmed and blessed the love and commitment they shared and recognized their marriage before God. As I pronounced them husband and wife, Karen opened her eyes and smiled. They shared a kiss, and there was not a dry eye in the room. We were on holy ground.

Karen moved to a hospice facility the next day and died within the week. I'll never forget Karen, Bill, and her family. I'll never forget the holy ground of Karen and Bill's wedding. My call to ministry was strengthened as I witnessed the resilience of Karen's spirit as she moved beyond her illness-ravaged body to her heart. Karen taught me the importance of helping patients connect with their hearts and, in that place of the heart, finding the holy ground of hope.

Practicing chaplaincy from my heart enables me to appreciate each person's beliefs and practices. I'm not called to challenge, proselytize, or judge. It is neither my place nor my desire to change anyone's faith. Rather, chaplaincy means meeting people where they are theologically and spiritually. It is my task to listen to and support patients, families, and staff as they find within themselves their own spiritual resources. What in someone's faith, beliefs, and practices will sustain, nurture, and contribute to their physical, emotional, and spiritual healing? How can my ministry of compassion, presence, and listening help call forth that spark of healing and hope, whatever faith (or none) is practiced?

I am fortunate that each day gives me opportunities to meet people who practice a wide variety of faith traditions. As Diana Eck wisely suggests, it is imperative that we engage with people who have different faiths from our own, and I believe that this urgency is foundational to Unitarian Universalism. It's also important to recall that Unitarian Universalism has a long history of appreciation and respect for the world's other religions. Fortunately, Unitarian Universalists have maintained our commitment to interfaith engagement, so much so that this value is included among our Sources: "The living tradition we share draws from many sources . . . [including] wisdom from the world's religions which inspires us in our ethical and spiritual life." Unitarian Universalism is the perfect theological starting point for my chaplaincy work because of this imperative to meet each interfaith encounter from my heart, where I am open to learning and growing as a person of faith.

Relying on my heart helped me when I was called early one morning to be with a family in the Heart Institute waiting room. I found two women who looked to be from India sitting there, their anxiety evident on their faces. I introduced myself and learned that their mother had suffered a heart attack and was having a cardiac intervention to try to open the blocked artery. They told me that their family was Hindu. I recalled my Hindu friends from the interfaith council and remembered what one of them said in a conversation about world religions: "There are many paths up the mountain. We all hope to arrive at the same destination." I found this family shared that openness as they welcomed my presence and prayers.

Their mother was taken from the Heart Institute to the Intensive Care Unit, where she was supported with a plethora of machines and medications. Despite these efforts, she was not doing well. More family began to arrive and I asked if they wanted me to contact the priest of the Hindu Temple and Cultural Center. They declined. Only a few hours passed before they were informed that the patient was living only because she was on life support. The family listened and agreed with the doctor that life support should be removed. After this conversation, one of the daughters left, going home to "get a few things." I remember feeling puzzled. Why would she go home now, with her mother so critically ill?

The daughter returned about an hour later, her mother was removed from life support, and her heart stopped beating almost immediately. The women of the family asked for assistance. They needed basins, washcloths, and soap to wash her body. I gathered these supplies and was then humbled and honored when they asked me to stay in the room and assist in the ritual. The atmosphere in the room was quiet and reverent, filled with love for this elderly woman. Few words were needed as we moved through the ritual washing. And then I learned why the daughter had left. She had gone home to get the sari her mother wanted to wear in death. The women of the family gently dressed her in her beautiful emerald-green silk sari. A family member had gone to the hospital gift shop and purchased a bouquet of apricot-colored roses, which they placed across her chest. The family then gathered around her to pray and say their goodbyes. The nurse who had been caring for her stepped close to me and whispered in my ear, "I have never seen a person look this beautiful after they have died." We stayed in that place of awe and beauty as she was taken from the room and the family left the hospital.

If I had been relying on my head, I might have missed the beauty. I might have wondered why anyone would go to this much trouble when only the body remains—an empty shell that would be cremated quickly. I am grateful that I leaned into my heart as this family included me in the quiet and reverent ritual of their loved one's death. I was on holy ground as I was challenged to a deeper understanding of beauty. I came to see that there is beauty even in death.

Working in an interfaith environment is truly one of the richest aspects of my work as a chaplain. Unitarian Universalism is a living tradition, meaning revelation is not sealed. We are called to live our Principles and Purposes and continue our theological growth. I learned quickly that interfaith engagement is not primarily a matter of intellectual learning. Nor does it mean just getting a good feeling, patting myself on the back, or affirming that I am a "good" Unitarian Universalist. Interfaith engagement involves taking the risk to get out of my theological comfort zone. It means being open and honest and willing to learn, knowing that my own faith may be touched, challenged, or changed. The interfaith relationships I have developed have helped me understand the difference between mere recognition or toleration of diversity and the richness of mutual understanding and transformation. This is why I have served for many years on the Greater Kansas City Interfaith Council. This is why I value so highly the interfaith aspect of chaplaincy. I know that working and engaging with people who practice faiths different from my own has led to relationships that have deepened my faith. In fact, one of my interfaith friendships led to an unexpected and deeply poignant experience of holy ground.

I was working a weekend shift at the hospital when I was paged to the Emergency Department for an incoming code blue, meaning that a patient required immediate resuscitation. The unit secretary quickly told me that there was a distraught family member with the patient. She hadn't wanted to leave his room and give the staff the space they needed to work. As I came around the corner, I saw my friend and colleague Mahnaz in the hallway just outside the treatment room. Mahnaz and her family are Muslim and we knew each other from working together at this Catholic hospital, where she had been a vice-president, and then from our work together on the interfaith council. My heart melted when I saw her. I held my friend, praying with her as the staff attempted to resuscitate her husband.

Their attempts were not successful. Mahnaz's husband, Farrukh, died that afternoon. He had just returned from the *hajj,* the pilgrimage Muslims are obligated to make once in their lifetime if at all possible. The first call I made on Mahnaz's behalf was to one of her closest friends, who was Jewish. Word of Farrukh's death spread quickly. The outpouring of support throughout the night of prayer and vigil was incredible. The next day friends and colleagues of many faiths attended Farrukh's funeral. After the service, we made our way to the graveside, where Mahnaz and Farrukh's two eldest sons lowered themselves into the grave to receive their father's body and place it in the ground. The eldest son, with arms stretched upward to receive his father's body, keened one prayer over and over, his voice raw with anguish and grief. The prayer was in Arabic, and I did not have to understand the words to be taken to that place of deep heartache and loss. This expression of grief was both particular and universal. The prayer was, as Leonard Cohen once sang, "a cold and a broken hallelujah." We transcended the particularities of religion and culture to come together on the common ground, the holy ground, of grief.

The experiences of holy ground that I have described continue to validate and deepen both my call to ministry and my understanding of how we find meaning in the face of vulnerability and suffering. My stories reflect a different and more difficult side of human reality than does Diana Eck's account of her experience in the Hindu temple. I was on holy ground in the hospital and at a graveside, not in a place of worship. These pastoral encounters occurred in places that embody vulnerability, places that acknowledge our human frailty and finitude. The Methodist minister William Bouton said it like this in a sermon: "We have often defined 'holy ground' as that place where we encounter God: On the barren soil of another's suffering—in the depth of [our own] or one another's need." My experience continually reinforces Bouton's words: Life is messy, full of uncertainty, and often unfair. And somehow we find meaning in these bleak and difficult places.

These are the themes I encountered when a call came from an administrative assistant in a nonclinical area of the hospital, asking me to come quickly to that area's conference room. Before I even stepped out of the hallway and into the office area, I heard someone wailing. Several people who worked in the area were standing outside the closed door of the conference room. They looked very relieved to see me and quickly told me that a police chaplain had just arrived to tell a young nursing student that her husband had died in an accident in another city. The nursing student was from Africa and had little family in the area. I took a deep breath, silently asked the universe to guide me, and stepped into the conference room.

The young woman was on the floor, crying and calling out her husband's name over and over. I sat next to her and offered the only thing I had to offer—my presence. Every fiber of this young woman's being was in pain. She rolled on the floor, her husband's name interspersed with the ultimate theological question: "Oh God, why, why, why?" There was, of course, no answer. Any words I said were like smoke, quickly dissipated by the intensity of her grief. In her vulnerability, she was totally unaware of her surroundings. I pushed tables and chairs out of the way, doing my best to create a place of safety as I entered into her rhythm of grief. At one point there was a knock on the door. The office staff could hear every cry, and it became clear that they had expected this wailing to stop once I arrived. They wanted her taken to the Emergency Department, where she would be given something to "calm her down." I knew this young woman was expressing her grief in a way that was appropriate to who she was. This outward expression of grief was what she needed. I closed the door and continued to sit with her, moving with her on the floor as her body rolled in waves of grief, holding her when she allowed me to.

After an hour or so, a cousin arrived. He sat with us, sometimes entering into her lament, but mostly listening to it. After a while she became quieter, the disbelief moving into exhaustion and emotional numbness. Without words, she agreed to let her cousin take her home. We half-carried her to his car. I said goodbye, slowly walked back to the office area, and sat with the staff for a while, letting them talk and debrief. The reality of being present with such strong emotion had touched us all. Rationality had no place here, where there were no words of comfort. It was a raw place of sweat, tears, and snot. My faith deepened as I entered this place of rawness, doing my best to create a place of safety for her to express her grief. This was holy ground because it was a place of pure and utter honesty, a place of the heart.

While our faith can deepen from standing on the holy ground of suffering and tragedy, let me be clear—I would never advocate seeking out suffering. Victor Frankl, who lived through the horrors of the Nazi concentration camps, wrote about his search for meaning in the midst of suffering. Although Frankl was able to find meaning while living through this heinous crime against humanity, he emphasizes that suffering is not the only way to find meaning in life. In *Man's Search for Meaning*, he writes, "If it [the suffering] is avoidable, the meaningful thing to do is to remove its cause, for unnecessary suffering is masochistic rather than heroic. If, on the other hand, one cannot change a situa-

tion that causes his suffering, he can still choose his attitude."
I absolutely agree. And I know there is never a guarantee that
anyone will learn or grow through suffering. All I know is that
I have been on the raw and bleak holy ground of my own and
others' suffering.

Being a chaplain means I sometimes struggle with the themes
of suffering and vulnerability. Dealing with sickness and tragedy
day after day can be emotionally and spiritually exhausting. On
a rational level, I don't understand why I was called to this ministry. I rail against suffering, and yet I am called to minister in
this place. The paradox of being comfortable in such an uncomfortable place baffles me. The best answer I have found comes
from the heart. The Unitarian feminist and Transcendentalist
Margaret Fuller had a favorite saying: "I accept the universe." I
interpret this to mean that although we cannot chose whether
or not we will suffer, we can choose our response. We can resist
the universe or accept it.

I remember when the concept of accepting the universe
became real for me. In my training as a chaplain, the other chaplains and I rotated on-call shifts, staying overnight at the hospital and dealing with any crises that occurred. When I started
doing on-calls, I was very anxious about what the night might
bring. Would a trauma come into the Emergency Department?
Would it be a code blue? Would it be a difficult death, with
family members either inconsolable or at each other's throats?
I tried to find some magic formula to prevent anything really
tough from happening on my shift. I tried to put a "hush" on
the hospital by thinking peaceful thoughts. I tried to just forget
that I was carrying the trauma pager. I tried sending up a quick
prayer—something really basic and desperate like "Please let
this be a quiet night." Well, saying the word "quiet" in a hospital is like a jinx. As you can imagine, none of this worked. Stuff
happens without any regard to my anxiety or what time of day
or night it is. And then, one night, something changed.

I arrived at the hospital for my on-call shift with my usual
anxiety about what the night might bring. And then, as I was
walking down the hall past the Emergency Department, heading into the ICU, something happened. Instead of resisting what

might happen, I felt myself enter into the flow of the hospital. It's hard to put into words—one moment I was standing on the outside, resisting everything that was happening, resisting both present and future. I can only describe the next moment as stepping into the river. Without thinking, I simply stepped off the bank and into the flow of all that was happening. It was pure, un-premeditated surrender. In that moment I became peaceful; I became part of the life of the hospital. I realized later that I had been operating from a place of fear and resistance. Once I stepped into the flow, there was no fear, only peace and acceptance. I knew that that night, and all nights in the future, I would deal with whatever might happen to the best of my ability. "Accept the universe" moved from theory to practice, from head to heart.

This attitude of acceptance became even more real when, soon afterward, I visited a dying patient. I had been visiting Dorothy for several weeks, and during that time her health continued to decline. It was clear she was dying. She was confined to bed, her arms propped up on pillows, her voice reduced to a whisper. The last time I visited Dorothy we talked briefly about where she was in her spiritual journey. Even though she could not move and could barely speak, her ice-blue eyes were clear and alive. Her voice was so weak that I couldn't hear what she said the first time she spoke. I leaned closer to hear her whisper, "Each day is what you make it."

I was on holy ground as I learned the true meaning of acceptance. Acceptance does not mean denying or diminishing life's suffering or the reality of death. And it certainly doesn't mean having a blindly optimistic "Pollyanna" attitude. Acceptance doesn't mean we have to like or be glad for everything that happens. Dorothy taught me that acceptance is not casual approval. Rather, it is the opposite of cynicism, hardheartedness, and bitterness. Acceptance means meeting all that life offers with courage, determination, and openness. Acceptance is holy ground because it defies reason; it is that beautiful place of being openhearted.

Acceptance of the universe is the attitude I need to meet the challenges of my work as a chaplain. I could never be fully and compassionately present with those who are suffering if I came to them with a hard, bitter, or angry heart. I strive each day to lead with my heart, to step into the river as I meet the unknowns each day inevitably brings. However, having worked in a Catholic hospital for more than a decade means I have been influenced by Roman Catholic beliefs and practices, particularly in my occasional use of confessional statements. In this confessional mode, I admit that there are days when I yearn for more contact with those who are theologically like-minded. There are days when I've had enough Jesus, enough traditional prayer, enough of hearing "God will never give you more than you can bear," "What doesn't kill you makes you stronger," or "Your baby died because God needed another angel." There are days when all I want is a good dose of Emerson or a few rousing verses of "Rank by Rank Again We Stand." In other words, accepting the universe, as I learned to do from Dorothy, isn't as easy as it sounds. Diana Eck had it right: Sometimes acceptance comes where we find ourselves challenged to a deeper faith.

One afternoon I was making a routine visit to a Baptist patient who had recently had major surgery. This was my first visit with him, and he engaged with me as soon as I introduced myself as a chaplain. He immediately asked me, "What would you say to God to make sure you would get into heaven?" I was surprised by his question and quickly ran through a few options in my head before deciding on a scriptural passage from Matthew that might satisfy both his need and my own religious integrity. I replied, "Jesus asked us to feed the hungry, visit the sick, and clothe those in need. I would say to God that I have tried to do what Jesus asked us to do for the least among us." I found out quickly that this answer did not satisfy him! He launched into a thorough discourse on faith and works. I listened as he gave me a lesson in salvation based on his Pauline theology. He believed in salvation by faith alone. Even though this is not a theology I share, my role as a chaplain is to meet patients where they are. I affirmed his theological perspective, and he concluded with a passage from Paul's letter to the Ephesians: "For by grace are ye saved through faith; and that not of yourselves: it is the gift of God: Not of works, lest any man should boast."

This visit left me feeling frustrated and angry. I felt I had missed the focus of the visit by taking the theological bait. It was also challenging because my theology doesn't include a traditional view of God or a belief in heaven beyond this life. What was really going on with this patient, I wondered? Did he doubt the strength of his own faith? Did he feel he had failed and his ill health was a punishment from God? Or perhaps this theological challenge was his way of taking control of his situation, a common need when major surgery comes unexpectedly and quickly. What frustrated me the most was that the visit had seemed to focus more on me than on the patient.

After I got home and started on my after-work walk with the dog, I continued to ponder what I could have done differently. It was a beautiful evening and I didn't realize that our walk to the park was perfectly timed to see one of the most beautiful and dramatic sunsets I have ever seen. I was stopped in my tracks by the beauty before me, and I suddenly knew what I would say to God (if there is a God) to ensure I would enter heaven (if there is a heaven). I would say, "Thank you! Thank you!" My anger and frustration were instantly replaced with a clear understanding of the theological challenge this patient had posed to my faith. I experienced one of those rare "aha!" moments as I realized the only adequate answer to the miracle of life, love, and beauty is gratitude. At that moment I experienced heaven; I was on holy ground.

I love my ministry in the hospital. Even with the vulnerability, the code blues, the unexpected deaths, even with the many variations on the theme of suffering, I am blessed in this ministry. In this often-difficult environment, there is the gift of profound connection. There is the gift of caring tenderly for those in that place where emotions are raw, that place where all social pretenses drop away and we meet human to human. There is the gift of witnessing and validating the resilience of the human spirit. This ministry with patients, families, and hospital staff nourishes my spirit and leaves its imprint on my heart. These places of the heart are holy ground.

And so I return one final time to the blessing in tongues I received from the Pentecostal patient and her pastor. This experience clarified the source of my faith. While ours is a faith of both head and heart, I now know that I lead with my heart. This is what my ministry as a chaplain is all about—connecting in that place where vulnerability, beauty, grief, love, and resilience find expression. And out of this deep place within myself, where emotions meet and merge, I have found the holiest of holy ground: gratitude. There is no other answer to this miracle of life and love. For the life I have been given, for my call to chaplaincy, for the sacred experience of working with those who are most vulnerable, for the love and resilience I have witnessed, for the many times I have been on holy ground, there is only one answer that is adequate: Thank you, thank you, thank you.

Lost (and Found) in Translation

NATHAN MESNIKOFF

During college, I took a year to study abroad in Japan. My first semester there I lived with a Japanese family. They spoke little English and I spoke almost no Japanese when we met that September. Still, we muddled through well enough. Throughout the fall my language skills rapidly improved and we all got used to doing much of our everyday chatting in simple Japanese. I enjoyed living in their tiny apartment home and I think they enjoyed getting to know this big (by their standards), hairy (by anyone's standards), American *gaijin* (foreigner). I came to feel nicely integrated into the family and that I had a solid, if basic, understanding of Japanese culture.

The semester flew by and winter break was upon me. New Year's Day is a major holiday in Japan, and I had gone out to participate in the revelry. I wandered the streets of the ancient city of Nara and visited one of my favorite temples, where there were huge kegs of *taruzake* (spiced rice wine) being generously ladled out. Huge bonfires lit the night and everyone seemed to be in an expansive, if not thoroughly inebriated, mood. The night progressed and more partying beckoned, but I needed to catch the last train back. I got home a little after midnight and was surprised and pleased to see guests were still there, happily chatting and snacking. I sat down and started talking with a cousin of my host mother. I was peckish, and seeing a small piece of cake left on a plate, I picked it up and ate it. The woman

I was speaking with smiled at me. I casually remarked, "*Watashi-wa itsu mo o'naka ga suita*" ("Oh, me, I'm always hungry")—not grammatically perfect, but I thought it would be understandable. Within moments of my uttering what I thought was a self-deprecating quip, conversation absolutely stopped around the table. The guests made their excuses and they all left. My host family was clearly very upset. I asked what was wrong; they responded with a torrent of Japanese. I had apparently embarrassed the family by implying that they didn't feed me enough. I was stunned. It hadn't occurred to me that my offhand comment could be understood as anything more than me poking fun at my own significant appetite. I said many times, trying to explain myself, that it was "*jodan dake deshita*" (only a joke). My host brother, eleven years old, was in tears. My host mother joined him. My host father, usually jovial and warm, was silent and stoic. I apologized repeatedly and even enlisted a professor at my university to help. Nothing helped. I moved out not long after; the relationship, sadly, was never repaired. It was just one short sentence, whose meaning I thought would be understood perfectly. I thought we had been speaking the same language. Clearly, something had gotten lost in translation.

A Unitarian Universalist Chaplain in the Evangelical Vatican

"Who better to be a hospital chaplain than a Unitarian Universalist?" I've heard this often from sympathetically minded people. Indeed, UU hospital chaplaincy makes sense to most of us within the tradition. We are, after all, open to the truth found in all authentic spiritual paths. We embrace diversity in many forms: spiritual, cultural, sexual, racial. And yet I have struggled at times as I seek to understand my ministry. How do I engage the patients, families, and staff I serve when so often we come from radically different theological and cultural places?

I live in Colorado Springs, one of the most conservative cities in the country, a place sometimes called the "evangelical Vatican." Me, I'm a Unitarian Universalist Buddhist Jew, not particularly theistic, deeply humanistic, and pretty far left socially and politically. How do I really listen and speak to someone who believes in original sin and vicarious atonement, and who takes the Bible literally? Am I being honest when I pray in the name of Jesus, or when I nod my head as others speak about the healing power of the blood of Christ or the importance of giving up all of one's problems to a God who knows all, heals all, judges all? What does it really mean to affirm people in beliefs that I fundamentally disagree with? Am I being honest with my patients? Am I being authentic to myself?

During graduate school, I was deeply influenced by the philosopher-linguists George Lakoff and Mark Johnson. Their book *Metaphors We Live By* examines how the metaphors we use not only reflect, but also shape, how we think about topics. Lakoff and Johnson point out, for example, that if the primary metaphorical structure you have for argument is war, then you will use language that reflects that underlying metaphor. You will talk about "shooting down" arguments, decide whether criticisms are "on target," and see people who are arguing as "attacking" and "defending" positions that may be "entrenched." Most importantly, such a metaphorical structure will frame the dialogue in terms of winners and losers, victory and defeat.

But one might imagine a different metaphorical structure. Another culture might understand argument as "dance." Members of such a culture might use very different language and think very differently about the engagement. They might see the participants as performers and focus more on their ability to lead or follow, to find a mutual rhythm and to perform in an aesthetically pleasing way, moving in time and in concert with one another. Looking on, many of us likely wouldn't even classify what was happening as an argument, since the basic metaphorical frame would be so different from ours. But the participants would still be seeking a way to resolve differences.

Metaphors allow us to concretize ideas so that we can relate to them more easily. Being embodied creatures, we seek to use embodied language to describe ethereal concepts. We talk of "spending" time, "falling" in love, and "losing" our minds. But time isn't actually money, love isn't a pool of water, and our minds can't be found with a GPS. And yet these powerful metaphors permeate our language, shape our conversations, and determine the course of our thoughts, and therefore of our culture and lives.

I found Lakoff and Johnson's insights meaningful both intellectually and spiritually. They made me more aware of the metaphors I was using and the power of language not only to express but to shape our thoughts about the world and our interactions within it.

As I worked my way through the four units (1600 hours) of Clinical Pastoral Education (CPE) usually expected of professional chaplains, I faced questions about my theology. How did I make sense of my clinical experiences, relate to my patients, and understand the work I did as ministry? As I said, I'm of mixed theological background and, like many Unitarian Universalists, don't have an elaborate, systematic theology. I didn't think of what I was doing in theological ways, because I'm not a theist. I don't have an overarching framework in the way most Christians do, at least theoretically. The philosophical underpinnings I do have feel highly personal and not universalizable —and I have no need for other people to share my specific beliefs, nor any interest in convincing them to do so. So as my chaplain colleagues spoke of being a conduit for God's love and grace, being the hands and feet of Jesus in the world, modeling their work after the work of their savior, or seeing the handiwork of God in each person's life, I found myself at a loss. The primary models of chaplaincy I heard were predicated on the existence of a being I didn't believe in or the work of a teacher I was sure had died two thousand years ago and hadn't come back. My chaplaincy reflects my core belief that whatever good will happen in this world, whatever solutions, whatever kindness, whatever comfort will come to the sick, the naked, or the imprisoned, must come from human beings, not through any divine intervention. I was inspired by humanistic philosophers, by the Buddhist ideal of compassion in action, and by a host of other spiritual influences, but not by a belief in any god or savior.

I went into chaplaincy because I was tired of the abstractions of academia. A direct, hands-on approach was to be the antidote for all the years I had spent in graduate school (almost ten by that point) living primarily in my head and estranged from my heart. I didn't want to build elaborate theologies of pastoral care; I just wanted to meet people where they were, hear their stories, and offer whatever comfort and solace I could by my presence. I wasn't interested in theological explanations, and certainly none that involved traditional Judeo-Christian beliefs. My perspective might have been well understood in a larger, more cosmopolitan or liberal city. But in Colorado Springs, I might as well have been speaking Japanese. This isn't to say that my supervisor or classmates were hostile, but I could tell that to many of them my views were foreign or even incomprehensible. Moreover, leaving aside the question of how I explain my chaplaincy to others, how do I explain it to myself?

In Translation

Ultimately, the most important question was how to connect where I was spiritually with where my patients were. My views weren't, after all, simply a variation on a common theme; they were in many ways diametrically opposed to it. This opposition is almost always apparent. At one of my first meetings with some of the volunteers in the spiritual care department in which I work, a volunteer asked which church I attended. When I replied, "A Unitarian Universalist one," and explained a little, she looked positively stricken. I feigned naiveté and asked what was wrong. She looked at me and said with intense concern, "Well, one of us isn't saved." I was sorely tempted to ask which one of us she meant, but I held my tongue. I have had many such encounters. I see the gap between their understandings and my own and wish to bridge it in some effective, authentic, and mutually honoring way.

Over time, I've begun to think of my chaplaincy through a metaphor of language: chaplaincy as translation. This metaphor works for me both because it structures the issue in a helpful way and because, having lived overseas for extended periods, I find it intuitive. I think it can be similarly intuitive to others who have struggled to learn foreign languages and cultures.

In addition to the fact that they can help me better connect with my patients, I have personal reasons for trying to learn these other languages. After all, the better we understand other languages, the better we understand our own. Studying a variety of foreign languages over the years—Latin, French, Hebrew, Spanish, German, Sanskrit, and Japanese—has helped me understand my native tongue in a way I never would have without these foreign perspectives. And the reverse is true as well. As anyone who has done translation work knows, the more you understand your own language, the more effectively you can translate others. This holds for the metaphorical translation work of chaplaincy as well—and after all, the *lingua franca* of chaplaincy is self-knowledge and awareness, which are routes to helping others. We examine ourselves in the process of CPE so that we can leave ourselves behind when we walk into a patient's room.

I seek to translate skillfully and mindfully because doing so helps me grow spiritually and professionally. But in the same way that, despite many years of studying a variety of languages, I speak only English with true fluency, I still may not thoroughly understand these other spiritual languages.

Can I speak evangelical Christian well enough to achieve genuine or even useful understanding with a patient? Can I listen, translating internally into language that makes more sense to me? Can I, for example, understand original sin to mean the fundamental, pervasive brokenness that I believe all human beings share—not condemning an innately flawed humanity, but compassionately recognizing that we all struggle with something, we all have cracks somewhere in our minds, hearts, and "souls"? Can I translate a belief in Jesus Christ as a personal savior into a desire to have a model for one's life, as a yearning for the clarity and help that I look for myself in my spiritual practices? Can I hear the frequent prayer for a miracle as a deep recognition of the seriousness of the situation and of human helplessness in the face of crisis?

I try. My translations are, inevitably, imperfect. But are they enough? Do they do more harm than good? What does it mean to reframe belief systems in terms of languages? How does doing so help me bridge the gaps between my worldview and theirs? How does this allow me to minister with authenticity and integrity? What gets lost—and, hopefully, found—in translation? I meet people, to the best of my ability, where they are, listening for their values and beliefs as a way of understanding their pain and suffering and, ideally, of connecting them with their strengths and sources of hope. I cannot understand completely, and so perhaps it is enough just to be a compassionate, nonanxious presence.

Over the years, many patients and families have assumed that I shared their beliefs. I think my skills as a chaplain (as a spiritual chameleon?) dovetail with their profound stress to create an effective and comforting illusion of alignment. This doesn't seem to be a significant functional problem, but it is important from what I might call an orientational perspective. For me to be happy with what I do, to feel fulfilled and satisfied, it is important that I understand how and why I do it. It is part of my spirituality to be intentional about my life, and so I want to have my chosen work align as much as possible with my deepest values, with my most fundamental orientation: my true north. I want to explore this metaphor of chaplaincy as a form of translation because it allows me to feel that I am doing my ministry in an intentional, considered way.

And despite my years of doing this work, I struggle with it from time to time because, at a deep level, I don't believe what many of my patients do. I find some of it ridiculous. Indeed, I find some of it offensive, if I am honest with myself. I try to understand why they believe as they do. I try to understand how these beliefs function in their lives and in their social settings. But still, when I check those beliefs against mine, a gap opens up between us. It feels like coming upon someone beaten in an alley. Imagine the poor soul lying there, bruised and battered, clearly in need of help. But you share no common language; you can't ask what hurts, who you should contact, what they need beyond the obvious. The victim speaks frantically, but you have no idea what they are trying to communicate.

I remember standing at the bedside of a young man, a boy, really. He was a foreign exchange student and had only been in the country a few weeks. He had never driven before, but decided to give it a try on the urging of some of his new friends. His first attempt ended tragically, leaving him with multiple severe injuries, including possible brain trauma. We were still working on getting his mother into the country, but his host mother rarely left his side. A woman of deep faith who felt overwhelmingly guilty for the grievous injury he had sustained under her care, she prayed for him constantly. Since she came from a Pentecostal tradition, her prayers would almost always includes long passages about being "washed in the blood of Jesus" or extensive admonitions to the devil to leave this child alone. She also clearly felt that this event was God's judgment upon her, a punishment for some spiritual failing.

This language was very foreign to me. It was not French or Spanish, with handy cognates I might latch on to. It was, to me, the spiritual equivalent of Tibetan or Swahili, languages for which I had little useful reference. I found the constant references to the blood of Jesus more than a little off-putting. They were so painfully literal, as were the commands to an actual sentient being named Lucifer. I didn't have any reference for this except horror movie caricatures.

The spirituality that makes sense to me is based on the assumption that we have access only to echoes of truths, like the reflection of the moon in a bucket of water—we cannot take those echoes literally, because the truths are more complicated than can be expressed in the crude structure of physical reality. Indeed, I've often said of the Bible that it is too important to be taken literally, and I feel that way about most spiritual utterances. They are the best we can do to capture the ineffable —that is what art, poetry, and mythology are for, to allow us sideways glimpses of transcendent realities. And yet here was a woman I was trying to help, speaking about the magical efficacy of the blood of a man dead for millennia and about a fallen angel who stalks us and concretely interferes in our lives. I felt lost. I had no meaningful way of understanding this language. I could, of course, have simply nodded my head and played along, but that would have felt disrespectful and would not have brought me closer to understanding her perspective and how I might help her in this struggle. Back to translation . . . and at this level of incomprehension I am forced beyond language, to the grunts, clicks, and barks of traumatic emotion and desperation, the tears and clutching hands that are what's left when our words fail us. And so often my most profound moments as a chaplain have been here, at the limits of language, where the intensity of experience moves us beyond the linguistic and theological abstractions that can divide us, and we are left with a shared humanity. I don't need to understand completely to feel her need for forgiveness and her hope for a young life that was entrusted to her and is now in an ICU.

Standing Somewhere

Some people, of course, might claim that my beliefs are irrelevant, as are perhaps even the beliefs of those I serve as a chaplain. My visits to patients theoretically exist in some kind of neutral supportive space and concern them, not me. Chaplains bracket out their own beliefs to be present to patients. And I can do that to a large extent—I can simply sit and listen intently, reflecting back their fears and hopes, serving as a mirror in which they can, hopefully, face their worries and see them in the context of their sources of hope and strength.

But as a professor of mine was fond of saying, "There's nowhere you can stand that isn't somewhere." Neutrality is an illusion. I can never be a perfectly clear window; I will always tint what passes through me with my inward colors. I will always hear through the echo chamber of my own attitudes and perspectives. So, despite my aspirations toward neutrality, I find myself returning to the metaphor of translation as a way of being more honest about my process as a chaplain.

Of course, the language metaphor breaks down somewhat when I consider the importance and functioning of belief and the ways that different faith stances are valued and judged. While one language may be more adept than another at expressing certain concepts, no one would claim that certain languages are "right" while others are "wrong." I don't believe that English is "better" than Japanese, or Hindi "better" than French. But I

do have beliefs about theologies. I believe that my spiritual perceptions and perspective are right. That's why I believe them.
No one willingly believes something they know to be wrong.
My patients believe what they do because they feel their beliefs
accord with reality. Their reasons for believing may be better
or worse. They may have simply inherited a belief structure, or
they may have studied extensively or had convincing religious
experiences that confirm their beliefs. One way or another,
though, they believe as they choose. And I do the same.

One might suggest that these differing judgments pose no
difficulty because I am a Unitarian Universalist and in my tradition we "bless all paths." But that doesn't mean we see no
differences between faiths. If we didn't, we'd have no cause to
exist—we'd simply go to the nearest religious community with
no regard to tradition or denomination: Baptist, Buddhist, or
Baha'i. Of course, we don't do this. We believe that our perspective is the correct one, at least for us, on matters of theology,
social justice, and organization. We honor the right of others
to choose differently. We respect that others both within and
outside our congregations may have different understandings of
reality. We believe that these differences don't have to separate
us into antagonistic camps.

The fact that I am comfortable with spiritual diversity, that I
have no problem reaching across the gap and translating others'
religious language into my own, doesn't mean my patients are
similarly comfortable. Does that matter? I have, on several occasions, taken communion in various Christian services, most
recently in a Catholic Mass when the priest, who well knew
my spiritual orientation, invited me to do so. I can enter into
this holy ritual full of my own understanding of what it means
to accept the most sacred into my own body, to see the transformation of simple bread and wine into divine substance and
to welcome and commune with it. But because I am at peace
with doing so doesn't mean that all those whose faiths I visit
would see my participation as respectful, or even as inoffensive.
I doubt the local bishop would be comfortable with a Buddhist
Unitarian Universalist Jew partaking in his most sacred ritual,
regardless of the sophistication of my metaphorical under-

standing. The parameters laid out by his faith tradition would be of central concern to him, not my spiritual flexibility. What boundaries between traditions do we need to respect?

From a chaplaincy perspective, it is a very short step from that question to this: How is accepting communion in a tradition outside my own different from praying in the name of a teacher who is not my personal savior? Maybe the difference is that the prayer is on behalf of someone who uses that language, who finds that metaphor structure important. Does that locus of intention matter? Is it okay just because I'm okay with it? Would my patient be okay with it? Is God okay with it, if she or he exists or has an opinion?

This is an old conversation. Philosophers and theologians have debated for ages what knowledge we can have of the world, let alone of the complexities of another's heart and mind. There is always a gap in understanding, and good chaplains maintain a constant awareness of this gap. Indeed, one of the first things we are taught is never to say, "I know how you feel." I don't know how you feel, or how you understand death or God. I don't know what this particular moment of suffering, which I happen to be present for, means to you in the context of your life and faith.

So I reach out across that gap and do three main things. First, I bear witness through unflinching presence. I don't turn away from your suffering, remorse, guilt, or anger. Second, I ask what this experience means to you. Where does this episode fit in the narrative of your life? Third, I try to help you connect with sources of strength and hope, whatever they may be: organized religion, disorganized religion, hiking, schnauzers, grandkids, whatever. Many people have no one who can effectively do these three things, these acts of human love and compassion. They require skills that many in our culture find difficult to master; it is hard to witness difficulties and suffering without intervening, trying to solve them, or feeling personally responsible for them. Too often we feel empathy—we feel what the other person feels. But empathy is frequently unhelpful. To be present every day, as I was in the ICU, to the truly horrific and undeserved injuries and illnesses of dozens and dozens of people, children and

adults—to hundreds of deaths—requires a careful management
of empathy. I bear witness to each crisis, but it isn't my crisis.

And so I practice focusing on sustainable compassion over
empathy, and now teach caregivers to do the same. But family
and friends, and even doctors and nurses, often find it difficult to
healthily separate themselves from the pain of others, and so they
don't venture into the wilderness with the patient, because they
fear getting lost themselves. Many of those who suffer feel—at
a deep, sometimes inchoate level—a sense of abandonment. But
the chaplain doesn't shy away, and the chaplain asks the questions few others want to ask or hear answered. What are you
afraid of? How do you feel about dying? What does this disease
or death actually mean to you, and how will your life be forever
changed by it? And often this is the most real work of translation we get to do as chaplains—ask these compassionate yet firm
queries about how the patient's personal story has changed.

Story is critical to emotional and spiritual health. Much of
my work these days is concerned with compassion fatigue and
secondary traumatic stress. At the core of this work lies the
simple truth that human beings live our lives through narrative. Language, as a trauma psychologist friend of mine says,
is the medium of thought, and so it is the means by which we
construct the meaning of our lives. The story that links our
past, present, and future is our conception of self. Who are we
without this story, these reference points? When trauma scatters
the mind and overburdens language, we are left with a gap, a
void in that narrative. Humans can withstand a lot, but the chaotic discontinuity of that void is too much, and so we fracture
and turn away. But the void will not be silenced. Like a tongue
constantly worrying at a gap in the teeth, our minds insist on
revisiting that hole over and over, often through nightmares and
flashbacks. Emotions that have not been expressed in language
intrude into the present and often cause tremendous suffering.
They must eventually find expression in language of one sort
or another. We must translate the raw data of experience into
coherent elements of story, so that the tale becomes a bridge
that enables our minds to pass over that experience, remembering without reliving, without stumbling or falling headlong into

dysfunction. Chaplaincy can help with this translation work as well, helping the individual give shape to words that reclaim the gaps. This translation does not occur between patient and chaplain; rather, the chaplain helps the patient translate, and thus better understand, their own experience. My understanding is secondary to my skill at exploring new metaphors and stories with my patient.

And yet, despite my willingness to wander in this desert with them, the meaning and context their suffering holds for them are hard for me to access. I don't believe people suffer as punishment for their sins—or at least not that this suffering is imposed by an external deity. I don't believe that we go to a paradise or a hell when we die. I don't believe that intercessory prayer is effective. But many of my patients believe all these things and more. They tell me their answers and I listen, and I hope I understand well enough to help and support them.

And, because I doubt I understand as well as I might or might need to, I translate. I take the idea of an externally imposed punishment and translate that into my own belief that our suffering is an internal construct—an interpretation of a painful experience. I take prayers to Jesus for healing and translate them into a way of safely voicing hopes and creating a sense of control (or at least a sense that someone benevolent is in control).

A Very Small House Indeed

Translation is seldom, if ever, a simple replacement of one word or concept by another. There is always nuance that is hard to capture, and skillful translation requires an idiomatic command of both tongues. I'm not sure I will ever be fluent in evangelical or Catholic. But I work on it as I can, slowly improving my ear, gradually getting better at seeing the nuances in the semiprivate individual languages of prayer, suffering, and meaning.

I'm reminded of Thoreau's comments in *Walden* on visitors and the distance needed between people for them to truly have a conversation. In the chapter titled, simply enough, "Visitors," he offers a series of rich metaphors for the requirements and challenges of genuine discourse:

One inconvenience I sometimes experienced in so small
a house, the difficulty of getting to a sufficient distance
from my guest when we began to utter the big thoughts
in big words. You want room for your thoughts to get into
sailing trim and run a course or two before they make
their port. . . . Individuals, like nations, must have suitable broad and natural boundaries, even a considerable
neutral ground, between them. I have found it a singular luxury to talk across the pond to a companion on the
opposite side. In my house we were so near that we could
not begin to hear—we could not speak low enough to be
heard; as when you throw two stones into calm water so
near that they break each other's undulations. If we are
merely loquacious and loud talkers, then we can afford
to stand very near together, cheek by jowl, and feel each
other's breath; but if we speak reservedly and thoughtfully, we want to be farther apart, that all animal heat and
moisture may have a chance to evaporate.

The hospital room is a very small house indeed. There is often
very little time or space to allow our thoughts the room they may
need to get into "sailing trim." Our "animal heat and moisture" sat-
urate the environment. We do what we can to create enough space
for the conversation to open sufficiently. But whether there is sufficient space or not, the chaplain enters into the storm of crisis and
does their best—sometimes offering a life preserver, a moment of
respite from the waves; sometimes serving as a lighthouse, helping those lost to orient themselves; and sometimes officiating at a
burial at sea for those who will never return to shore. Pastoral conversations often have a maritime quality. Patients may tack back
and forth as they try to make headway toward a painful idea. Difficult issues may be submerged under the weight of denial, only
to surface again, buoyed by the psychic pain they inflict and the
human need to make sense of such pain. And in these private
depths, my experience is that all faiths become strongly individual. No truly common language may exist for the singular experience of profound suffering and loss. No one speaks this unique
dialect of Christianity, or Judaism, or Hinduism.

Translation occurs not just between chaplains and patients; chaplains also help patients translate with themselves. I, being familiar with both the language of spirituality and the language of crisis or anger or suffering, help the patient translate what might have seemed like babble ("like Babel") into comprehensible utterances, deciphering a story that now holds meaning. Here my lack of fluency in a particular faith language may even be an asset. Since I have little commitment to a particular linguistic frame, I can sometimes help the patient find their way into a different metaphorical structure. Indeed, sometimes my job is to challenge a language that has run out of words, become too constrictive, too restrictive to let people fully express themselves.

Mistranslation is always a risk—and I may never realize my errors. There is no translator in the room who can adjust my accent or clarify my remarks. I watch, of course, as I did in Japan and in other lands, where my language skills were imperfect or nil, for the other cues: a smile, the deep sigh of released tension, the hand outstretched in appreciation of my presence. And yet I wonder about what gaps in understanding remain.

And, like literal translation, spiritual translation has many levels. A fellow chaplain pointed out to me the cultural and historical overlays on an already complex theological landscape. As an African American, she noted that when some of my patients' families speak of their loved one going to "a better place" they may not just be referencing a concept of heaven but also, perhaps unconsciously, connecting to the tragedies and suffering of slavery. I will never translate perfectly—the human and individual experience is too complex, too layered.

And so I listen as my patients speak their hopes and fears, their angers and joys into the space between us, translating their theological views into ones that I can understand, access, manipulate. I can then re-present these back to the patient, filtered through my perspective, a perspective tempered by emotional and temporal distance, and hopefully communicating my presence, compassion, courage, and desire to help. I muddle along, as I did in Japan, mostly being understood, sometimes not—but I try, as best I can, to communicate authentically.

My persistent hope, suspicion, and experience is that a shared humanity suffices. I spend so little time discussing theology and so much just listening to people's pain and fear, their hope and peace. We chaplains speak of a "ministry of presence." Maybe that is sufficient, or at least the best I can offer. There is, after all, an implicit spiritual relativism in chaplaincy if we're honest—and perhaps even a bit (or more than a bit) of quasi-Universalism. I spoke with several colleagues, poking, prodding, and trying to understand what they really thought about other religions. Most come to a place where they abandon the issue to God. But most also respect and appreciate paths other than their own. How can you be an effective chaplain if you genuinely have no respect for the patients' beliefs? My concept of translation at least lets me hear their beliefs and place them, no matter how foreign they may be to me, in a framework that allows me to appreciate their function, if not their form.

Alternatives: Shepherd or Parent?

As an alternative to translation, what other metaphors might be used? Chaplaincy as shepherding? I know that is a metaphor Jesus himself used, but I don't like what it implies about the abilities of those to whom I minister, nor the suggestion that I know their safest route home or can keep the wolves at bay. And I don't think the metaphor of shepherding structures my experience of chaplaincy in a way that deepens my connection to patients and honors their own wisdom. Shepherding and other similar metaphors for chaplaincy often assign a privileged position to chaplains and their supposed wisdom—a position I'm not sure is due me. Such a position may be more appropriate to parish ministers and other settled clergy, who are, in most traditions, seen explicitly as a guide for the perplexed, offering instruction in how to walk the path of a particular tradition.

Moreover, in my experience, many people aren't looking for a shepherd, and those who are don't always find one to be useful. I am often reminded of Herman Hesse's characterization of Siddhartha, in the book of the same name, who reflects that "knowledge can be communicated, but not wisdom." The breakthroughs my patients have are almost always a result of their own work, not mine—I can companion them, but I can't carry their burden any appreciable distance.

There are other metaphorical structures we might look to for understanding the work of the chaplain. The metaphor of the chaplain or minister as parent certainly has a long history; some traditions even refer to their clergy as "father." But while this is perhaps better than the image of the chaplain as shepherd (at least I and my patients are now the same species), it still implies strongly that authority and wisdom lie with the chaplain. And, again, while that may be appropriate to the settled clergy of certain traditions, it doesn't resonate with my experience of being a hospital chaplain.

I'm mixing metaphors a bit here, or at least going back and forth between categories. The concept of a shepherd or parent focuses on a subject, on how the chaplain might identify, while the concept of translation focuses on an activity. And I think this is appropriate; it allows me to focus more on the dialogical quality of chaplain-patient interactions and on the work that gets done in them. I'm reminded here of the theologian Carter Heyward's concept of "Godding." The chaplain-patient relationship is centered on mutuality and a co-creation of meaning and hope. This flattening of authority seems more appropriate to the work of pastoral care.

The Limits of Authority and the Problems of Comparison

I lean away from authority-laden metaphors because I don't think good chaplains work that way. While I certainly feel that my ministerial authority gives me the right to enter the room and ask difficult questions, I don't think that authority extends to defining the answers. I know this belief makes sense within a Unitarian Universalist theology, especially with our concern (to put it mildly) about hierarchy and paternalistic authority, but I see it in good chaplains of all backgrounds. Suffering is certainly a universal experience, but it is also profoundly unique, just as everyone has fingerprints but each set are particular to the individual. I prefer to see my work as translation rather than leading or advising because I genuinely believe that each individual is on a unique journey. For me to respect that journey, I have to take their expressions of faith as unique, and honor them by seeing them not as dogmas to be slotted into particular stages or categories (though such theoretical models may be helpful in the work of translation), but as the personal autobiographical expressions they are. And isn't that at the heart of Unitarian Universalist theology—that we appreciate and celebrate our common humanity while allowing each individual to find their own unique path to wholeness?

It's for this reason that I dislike the metaphor so often used for interfaith communication: that we are all climbing one mountain but on multiple paths to the summit. It fails to honor particularity enough, across either traditions or individuals. We are too often too ready to conflate vaguely similar structures within different traditions—to find analogues when we really should be focusing on dialogues. For example, we see that both Buddhism and Christianity have a teleological element, a goal, and so we equate nirvana with heaven. And yet they are quite different. Heaven, at least as traditionally understood, is a place where one's soul goes after a good and— often more importantly—faithful life. Nirvana isn't a place, and in any event Buddhism has no conception of a soul that could go anywhere; if anything, nirvana is an extinguishing of that ego energy that careens from life to life like the energy transmitted from billiard ball to billiard ball across an infinite table. The impact provides impetus to move the next ball, but the cue ball doesn't turn into the eight ball. The metaphor of one mountain, many paths glosses over these differences in a comforting, but unacceptably homogenizing and often pejorative or paternalistic, way, however well intentioned it is. Religions aren't equations to be balanced and reduced to their common factors. A more apt analogy is that there are many mountains, many paths, and one universal human urge to climb. These two theological concepts are not the same, not even neighbors, probably not even in the same hemisphere.

Shifting the metaphor shifts our understanding and potentially our practice.

The Risk of Grayscale

But the metaphor of translation itself risks the problem I'm trying to avoid. I do not take what the patient says at face value,
on its own; rather, I turn it into something that is comprehensible to me but would be incomprehensible to the speaker. I
guess that's a risk of translation. I'm not sure what other choice I
have. I don't believe in the basic theological tenets of Christianity. I can take them at face value, as mere story constructs that I
can comprehend narratively, but that denudes them of impact.
It's like taking a brilliantly colored picture and turning it into
grayscale; I'll see the outlines but little of the richness. In translating, I take value statements that have tremendous import
and weight for the patient and turn them into value statements
of tremendous import and weight for me, and then I use that
translation to minister. I acknowledge that translation isn't an
exact science, but it allows me, as an outsider to the patient's
understanding (as I think we mostly always are to each other
at some level), to access not the literal value of their speech
but the impact value of their intention. And this is my ultimate
aim as a chaplain: to hear, beneath the plain value and theological orthodoxy, the impact that this experience is having on the
person. Not to do anything with it, but to bear witness to their
journey and, in bearing that witness, to help lend it dignity, to
help them find their own meaning and path, and to reflect back
the deep worth that their own unique language has.

    In the end, I have to hope that what gets lost in translation
isn't ultimately as important as what gets found in translation.
I have to hope that the specific theological concept—such as
heaven, or prayer, or even God—isn't as important as the meaning it holds for the patient. And I use high-stakes examples of
what can get lost because I know how imperfect my translation
can be. But I will never be able to really understand what a belief
in heaven provides or how an incarnation of God could affect a
specific event in my life. I'm just not wired that way, spiritually.

But because I feel called to ministry, and in particular to hospital chaplaincy, I choose to engage in an honest effort at translation, hoping to preserve the impact of a belief when its literal meaning is inaccessible to me. As Herman Melville suggests in a letter to Nathaniel Hawthorne, "Let us speak, though we show all our faults and weaknesses,—for it is a sign of strength to be weak, to know it, and out with it,—not in [a] set way and ostentatiously, though, but incidentally and without premeditation." I may make manifest my gaps in understanding every time I engage with someone of a different faith, but I'd rather do that than remain fearfully silent or abandon this ministry.

So what I hope gets found in translation is what I believe to be ultimately true—that we may never really understand each other, but it is critically important to try. The presence, even in and among the mistranslations, is more important than complete understanding. The presence and intention are perhaps more important because I don't want to assume you and I are speaking the same language. When I do make that assumption, I fear I am less attentive to the minute particularities of your experience because I am presuming that I actually know what you're saying, when that may not be true at all. I'd rather assume that you are foreign to me, speaking with an accent I have to work to comprehend. This sharpens my attentiveness, makes me slow down my listening and hopefully hear what you are really trying to say. And isn't this what we try to do as chaplains: to hear deeply, fully, and compassionately even if we aren't having the same experience of sadness, loss, hope, or joy that the patient is at that moment? To be fully present, without assuming that we know exactly what they are going through, exactly what they are saying. In the end, I believe this presence—this full human honoring without assumptions, this appreciation without complete understanding, but full of love and compassion —is what gets found in translation.

Personhood and Interdependence— Caring for Those with Dementia

ANDREW TRIPP

Unitarian Universalism provides abundant resources for those who are cognitively able. We Unitarian Universalists inherit a great legacy of education and learning, with historical ties to many world-renowned centers of higher education. Sermons and faith development programs in UU churches often are deeply researched and assume considerable intellect and sophistication among our membership. According to data reported by the Unitarian Universalist Association in 2008, rates of college graduation and postgraduate education among adult Unitarian Universalists are twice the national average. However, our de facto cognitive ableism—the idea that one must have relatively high cognitive function to participate in and receive the ministry of Unitarian Universalism—is not necessary in Unitarian Universalist chaplaincy. Unitarian Universalism provides chaplaincy resources for patients and families living with dementia by focusing on the First and Seventh Principles: the inherent worth and dignity of each person, and respect for the interdependent web of all life. These Principles orient chaplains, as well as other UU caregivers, to care for those living with dementia, encouraging them to maintain openness and to discern what kind of ministry will be effective in each encounter. Compassionate care improves when chaplains treat each person with dignity, recognizing our interdependence.

My first week in hospice chaplaincy presented a steep learning curve. My coursework in pastoral care and counseling, as well as my Clinical Pastoral Education (CPE) units, offered me resources that relied on the patients' ability to share stories and other ways to make meaning in the midst of struggle and pain. However, during my first week of hospice chaplaincy I met several patients with terminal dementia who could not engage in meaning making through discussion. They challenged my skills and training as a chaplain, as well as my unspoken cognitive ableism and educational privilege, which had been nurtured through my experience and formation in Unitarian Universalism. I also witnessed how dementia disrupts relationships between people living with it and their loved ones. Families, friends, loved ones, and caregivers emotionally suffer when the person living with dementia begins to forget them. People living with dementia suffer as well, when caregivers and loved ones approach with questions such as "Don't you remember me?" or "What is my name?" that reinforce feelings of estrangement and inferiority. Time after time, I saw such patients, who primarily lived in assisted living facilities and nursing homes, receive fewer and fewer visits from their family members as their dementia progressed because the visits became too painful for their family members. Some loved ones of patients stop visiting, stating that the person they knew is already gone.

My first spiritual assessment of a hospice patient with a dementia diagnosis was a spectacular disaster. At the time, I was unaware of the Medicare guidelines for terminal dementia, which specify that a person who can speak no more than six words in a coherent sentence is eligible for a terminal dementia diagnosis. The patient was in a wheelchair at that point, and I wheeled her to a quiet room in her assisted living facility so we could talk. I began the spiritual assessment with open-ended questions like "Tell me about your experience with religion" and "What is important to you?" and she looked at me with growing pain on her face and only responded with "I don't know about that" and "I didn't think about that." I soon realized, from her facial expressions and body language, that my questions upset her and reminded her of her cognitive decline.

With each question, I reinforced the cognitive divide between the two of us. Our conversation showed me how unhelpful, and potentially counterproductive, standard chaplaincy questions could be with terminal dementia patients. Her health care proxy informed me of her religious tradition, but the patient could not share her sources of spiritual strength and meaning making with me. I left the encounter doubting that my time with her could become meaningful and effective ministry. This humbling encounter sent me on a path to learning alternative approaches to chaplaincy with those living with terminal dementia. I began with learning more about dementia, before learning how to meaningfully engage with patients and their loved ones who faced the disease.

As time passed with this woman in my care, I noticed that she would make the sign of the cross repeatedly when she was by herself. Her signing inspired me to bring in rosary beads for her to hold, and she would follow along when I would pray the rosary with her. She smiled and her body language indicated increased peace and calm when I held or massaged her hand. Certain songs, especially those that had been popular in her younger years, elicited positive responses from her every time she heard them. The facility brought in animals as part of its recreation program, and she glowed every time she held a dog or cat. As her dementia progressed, she sometimes had dramatic mood swings, but since she had taught me about these interests of hers I knew how to soothe her when she sobbed. My ministry of presence became essential to her care. Once I was authentically present to the cues she offered, she could teach me what was effective for her pastoral care. The initial spiritual assessment acted as a barrier between us, since I focused on information I needed instead of paying attention to what the woman offered. While being authentically present with her took much longer than quickly obtaining answers to questions, my presence taught me about her deeper spiritual strengths and needs.

This patient brought me back to the First and Seventh Principles of our Unitarian Universalist faith, helping me see them as spiritual and theological resources for chaplaincy. The two Principles not only state liberal religious values, but are also deeply spiritual and meaningful in our relationships with one another. Chaplaincy is about caring for and attending to the spiritual needs of the people in our care. It is a profession of relationships.

Our First Principle, affirming the inherent worth and dignity of every person, is much more than a general acknowledgment of human value. We proclaim as a faith statement that there is intrinsic dignity in every person. When someone is in cognitive decline, she has no less personhood than she did when she possessed her original cognitive functioning. The goodness of a person cannot be marred by the diminishment of their cognitive capacity. Every person has dignity and worth, which are not contingent upon ability. When we lose sight of the inherent worth and dignity of people, our capacity for cruelty grows. I had a bedbound patient with dementia, who was in a facility because she could not live at home. She had become deaf later in her life and never learned sign language, which meant communication was even more of a challenge. At times she could read single words written on a whiteboard, but most of the time she could not do even this. In the last two years of her life, only one of her adult children came to visit her. She was lonely, and while she couldn't speak, she was able to cry. I often heard her sobbing as I approached her room, but she usually stopped crying and smiled when I came to visit. I held her hand and offered to massage it. She laughed and smiled when I picked up her stuffed animals, dancing them and playing with them for her. She would hug them when I held them to her chest. Without words, we could recognize our care for one another, which was rooted in my understanding of her fundamental dignity and worth. After she died, at her calling hours, I met with her two sons, who had not visited with her in the last years of her life. Without much prompting, they shared their feelings of guilt, sadness, and loss. They both said seeing her in her hospital bed had been painful, but they both wished they had seen her at least one last time.

The Seventh Principle, respect for the interdependent web of all existence of which we are a part, also provides chaplains with an important resource for caring for those with dementia.

Unitarian Universalists often use the Seventh Principle to speak of ecology and of living lightly on the earth, but it has a deeper and more profound meaning. The vision of the interdependent web offers us a vision both of current relationship and of future flourishing and thriving as we more fully embrace that web. We all are enmeshed in relationship with each other, and we are dependent upon one another as we are dependent upon and in relationship with our natural world. We can honor people's dignity and worth only in the midst of relationship and care.

One of my patients was a very educated and intelligent man before dementia struck. He had been a university professor and dean, and was married to a professor. By the time he came into hospice, he could only walk if someone held his hand. And his speech was mostly incoherent. My first few visits with him left me feeling unsatisfied, since he could not tell me what still gave him comfort. I held his hand and we would walk around the floor of his facility, since he became anxious in group activities and was easily overstimulated. Once when I visited him during breakfast I saw him tapping his toe to the beat of the music that was playing, and so I began to play him music during our visits. I spoke with his wife, who told me that he still loved classical music, Welsh hymns and chorales, and old church artwork. I played him symphonies from my smartphone and Welsh music through YouTube. On hearing the music, he would stop what he was doing and wave his arms as if conducting. For up to ten minutes at a time he would stay in a single spot instead of moving restlessly about, and he smiled as he conducted. I showed him pictures of stained glass, and he would trace his finger along the patterns. Then we would go for a walk, and often he was more lucid after the music than before. On one of his last lucid days with me, he stopped me while we were walking and said to me, "It is such a kind thing you do with me."

His facility offered wonderful activities designed for people with dementia, but the staff did not have the time to relate to him one on one, as he needed. In his last days he was bedbound and mostly asleep. His wife sat vigil with him, and when I was in the facility I sat in his room with them. I shared with her the good times he and I had been able to have, even with his dementia. She shared how her choir had come in and sung for him, bringing a smile to his face in his last days. We ministered to one another as we sat vigil, and we felt the tangible healing power of our relationship. I was grateful that she had given me tools to relate meaningfully to him. She was grateful that I had been there, spending one-on-one time with him. We were both grateful for his presence in our lives, both richer for having been in relationship with him.

Chaplaincy from the Unitarian Universalist faith perspective requires both caring for the person living with dementia and healing the web of interrelation. Chaplaincy in this context reminds people living with dementia of their dignity, improves their quality of life, and helps restore their relationships with their loved ones.

Being present with someone is one of the simplest ways of caring, yet one of the chaplain's most difficult spiritual practices. Someone who is authentically present focuses not on their own needs as a caregiver, or on the efficacy of what they do or say, but rather on the person they are with. Witnessing the personhood of another requires spiritual centeredness; we must set aside our own fears and concerns so the fullness of the other can speak. Attending to someone living with dementia can be uncomfortable because dementia demonstrates that we are all only currently able, and that disability can come upon any of us. Similarly, we become uncomfortable when someone's cognitive decline means our normal ways of conversing with and caring for them are no longer effective. Chaplains must have the spiritual centeredness to honor and acknowledge this discomfort, but then set those feelings aside to encounter the person who is present and in need of care.

Pastoral presence entails preparation. People with dementia lose the capacity to answer open-ended questions or summarize their lives, but long-term memory lasts well into dementia's progression. Loved ones can share meaningful stories from the patient's life, allowing the chaplain to learn about the person, and their loved ones to enter into their care. Learning such stories provides the pastoral caregiver with opportunities to engage with the patient by sharing their story back to them. Important events like weddings, births, and educational and professional achievements hold bundled memories about preparation, relationships, and effort, and remind the person of more than just the single event. Sharing these stories takes the person back to happier days. Authentic presence includes witnessing the person's life back to them, acknowledging the importance of their accomplishments. In this manner, you let them know that they are not forgotten, and that you care enough about their dignity to remember their story.

Like stories about important events, favorite songs are tied to multiple and complex memories. Music brings back not just a melody and lyrics, but also cherished reminiscence. The sections of the brain that respond to music are different from those that respond to speech, so an encounter that involves both speech and music stimulates more of the brain. Many studies show that music, particularly music that people with dementia already know, increases quality of life by soothing their agitation, promoting their appetite, better orienting them to reality, and improving their ability to engage with others. People who participated in organized religion will associate music from their tradition with memories of holidays, rites of passage, and the rhythm of religious participation. Providing such music stimulates their deeply held memories, allowing them to remember and relive meaningful moments while also connecting with their spiritual life. Similarly, music from people's younger years brings back memories and improves their quality of life. Patients in wheelchairs who have not spoken to me in weeks have lit up when I played them music from their twenties and thirties, and have danced in their chairs to the beat of the songs. Pastoral care and meaning making include providing people with moments of joy and delight.

One of my patients came into hospice very weak and frail. She lacked the abdominal strength to even sit up in a wheelchair, so she had to be in a geriatric recliner. In her younger years, she had been a missionary in Japan, and pictures of Japan hung on the walls of her room. Her daughter also told me she was a huge fan of Roy Orbison and of "Country Roads" by John Denver. She enjoyed hearing me tell her about her experiences in Japan, since she could no longer share her experiences but remembered them when she was reminded of them. When I played her "Pretty Woman," "You Got It," or "Country Roads," her whole face lit up and she would sing along and move her hands and feet to the beat of the song. She would smile the rest of the visit, and would become more engaged and more talkative than before the music. During her last few days of life, she was asleep and could not be woken by gentle touch or by voice. During those days, when I played the Roy Orbison and Friends *A Black and White Night* album for her, her breathing deepened and became more peaceful, indicating that on some level she understood and appreciated the music. Interestingly, even though she had been a missionary, traditional sacred music did not elicit the same response. Being present and open to what was meaningful and spiritual for her gave me tools to provide her with proper care, which I would not have been able to do if I had assumed that I knew, on the basis of her missionary work, what she would find meaningful.

Pastoral presence, shared storytelling, and music provide people living with dementia with reminders of their dignity, worth, and moments of joy. However, their loved ones also need care to restore their relationships and improve their interactions with them. Unlike diseases that bring a faster decline, dementia can, over time, change the personalities of people afflicted with it. They forget their loved ones and gradually respond less and less often, either with speech or body language, to anything their loved ones do or say. Each decline brings a new loss to their loved ones and caregivers, so that they feel anticipatory grief for the losses to come, as well as present grief for the losses that have already happened. People experiencing anticipatory grief may begin to detach from their loved one, to protect their own feelings. They may rehearse the person's death, so that when it happens they will be more prepared. Caring for parents, especially, can evoke complicated emotions, including resentment and anger. Many people find such feelings socially unacceptable and need external permission from a chaplain to admit their anger, frustration, and sadness. As they work through these emotions, chaplains can help them acknowledge that their feelings are so profound because their relationship with their loved one is meaningful and important.

Unitarian Universalist understandings of personhood and interdependence encourage communities to thrive and flourish. How we honor and acknowledge those who are weak and silenced speaks to how we honor and acknowledge the whole of existence. Encountering the painful aspects of existence by affirming dignity and joy, and acknowledging human worth allows Unitarian Universalist chaplains to demonstrate the transformative power of spiritual care. Chaplaincy based on Unitarian Universalist perspectives on personal meaning making, authentic presence and companionship, and genuine concern for relationships can transform the lives of those living with dementia. Our work for right relationships, our work for compassion, and our work for human dignity do not need to end when a person can no longer speak eloquently or converse deeply.

Suffering, Faith, and Hope at a Children's Hospital

KAREN B. TALIESIN

It was my second day as a full-time chaplain at a pediatric hospital. Heading up from my office to the patient units, I walked to the Forest Zone—by way of the River and Mountain Zones—and onto the cancer care unit to visit a five-year-old girl just admitted the day before. As I knocked softly on the door, I saw a little girl—the patient—sitting up in bed, playing with some toys. Her mother was lying on the couch against the wall resting, her arm over her eyes.

The little girl looked up at me, her bright eyes fairly dancing, and said, "Hi! Who are you?" I knew there was no way she would know what a chaplain was, and all too late I realized I had no idea how to explain to a five-year-old what it is a chaplain does. So I stammered out, "I'm Karen . . . and I come by sometimes to see how you're doing . . . here in the hospital. I just want to know how you're feeling . . . in your heart. . . ." As I said this, I wondered if she was even able to understand that much, so I started to say more—but she interrupted me, saying, "Oh. I have cancer. My brother says I could die. . . . Do you know when the snack cart is coming?"

I felt my heart skip a beat. As I took a second to catch my breath, I heard a gasp, then a sob, coming from the couch. Her mother had been awake enough to hear what her daughter had said. It was at that moment that I began to realize it's the children who lead us adults through this overwhelming and devastating journey through cancer and illness, injury and trauma, disease and heartbreak. For though I was to spend the next few months occasionally talking and playing with this sweet girl, it was her mother who needed spiritual care and support. It was her mother who questioned the cancer, the lack of a cure, the cruel hand of fate or karma, and, most vehemently, her god.

And the little girl? She rarely questioned anything other than when the snack cart was due. So I spent the next year ministering mostly to her mother and father. In the end, when this little one breathed her last, she was surrounded by family and friends, wrapped in the arms of her parents, her room a blaze of love, that dancing light in her eyes forever imprinted on our hearts.

At the pediatric hospital where I work, there is a small team of chaplains who provide respectful spiritual care to patients, families, and staff of all faiths and spiritualities, including those who identify themselves as nonreligious or nonspiritual. Chaplains are available to meet urgent spiritual and emotional needs; to lead worship services, meditation sessions, and educational classes; to help people connect with local faith or spiritual communities; and to provide sacred texts, inspirational and self-help literature, and other spiritual resources. Chaplains are available day and night, around the clock and throughout the weekend. Anytime anyone needs support—including staff members— they simply ask the nurse to page the on-call chaplain and one will arrive to provide spiritual care.

But what does it mean to "provide spiritual care"? Spirituality, very basically, is the way we all experience life by striving to make meaning, to find hope, and to feel safe. How do we make meaning of the good things as well as the difficult things that happen to us? Do we rely on friends, family, Allah, Jesus, God, universal love, or a walk in the woods? When we're overwhelmed, what we once relied on may not help us, and we may experience spiritual and emotional chaos, pain, and distress. Adults may be in spiritual chaos or pain when what they lean on—their family, their work, their god—fails them, not providing the answers, solutions, or hope they so desperately need.

A while ago, I visited with a mother whose eight-month-old baby boy had Down syndrome. He was in the hospital for a respiratory infection and was doing fine, but the mother had requested a chaplain, as she was still struggling with accepting all she had been handed when her son came into her life. She told me, "I'm a 'Type-A' personality—everything has always been perfect for me. When I was pregnant with him, I spent an hour in prayer every morning to ensure that this baby would be born healthy. I don't drink, I don't smoke, I eat right, I exercise. Why did this happen?"

For quite some time, I listened to her ask "why," her pain—her spiritual pain—evident on her face and in her voice. As I listened, I heard in her words my own litany around my personal struggles. How many times do I, like parents and patients, ask, "Why is this happening to me?"

As I listened to this mother's words of pain and longing, the words that came to me were "I hear what you're asking, and I know I ask the 'why' question, too. But I've never heard a good answer to that question. I wonder if we're asking the wrong question. I wonder if our energy would be better spent asking 'how'? How do we live with what we've been given? How are you going to love and care for this child?" The mother took this in, then began to smile. "Yes," she said, "I believe that's right—it's the how and not the why. Figuring out the why doesn't really help me. My work is to figure out the how." Now I see this mom and her son periodically when they come in for clinic appointments. She is loving and caring and even joyful with her sweet son. They are both well and happy and figuring out the how just fine.

Spiritual pain in children may arise when they feel lonely, confused, or scared, or when they are worried about their parents. A child in spiritual pain makes me think of a nine-year-old girl I'll call Kelsie who was diagnosed with cancer. Her family lived in Montana, and they would come to the hospital for months at a time in order for Kelsie to receive treatment. Early in her treatment, Kelsie's father brought her to see me in my office.

Kelsie appeared quite shy, so I suggested we go into the chapel to take a look around. In the chapel, she stopped and looked at the scripture books on a shelf. She touched the Qur'an and the Tanach, walked to the prayer book where families write their prayers, walked by the piano touching some of the keys, then by the meditation benches. She noticed the four directions— North, South, East, and West—painted on the ceiling, and the prayer rugs for Muslims that lay over some of the chairs.

Kelsie was so quiet and thoughtful that I sat down and simply watched as she made her way around the chapel. Eventually, she came to the memorial book, in which is written the name of every child who has died at the hospital. Then she walked over to where I was sitting and climbed up in my lap. I wrapped my arms around her and held her close. We said nothing for a long time, simply sat, each feeling the heartbeat of the other. After a while, she whispered, "My tumors haunt me."

Children are rarely able to express their spiritual pain, either because they don't have the words or because they don't want to worry their parents and other loved ones. All too often after a child puts words to their feelings, an adult will jump in with words that are meant to soothe or placate. They say things like "It will be okay," "We're going to fight this," "God has a plan," and "God doesn't give you more than you can handle." These kinds of phrases tend to imply to the child that it's best not to talk about their difficult feelings. Words and phrases of comfort used too soon, before the child's pain and feelings are heard and acknowledged, primarily indicate the adult's discomfort with the child's feelings. Such attempts to make the child feel better simply shut the child down. Often the best—and sometimes the hardest—thing to do is to provide time and silence for the child to process their feelings and find the words to express them.

After Kelsie told me her tumors haunted her, I continued to hold her, as there was nothing to say. We sat for a while in silence. Then I whispered into her ear, "I love you, and I'm here for you." Then I talked to her about the breath prayer, a prayer you can compose to say over and over, in rhythm with your breathing, that may help when things are scary or sad. Kelsie told me she would like to try it, and when I asked her what phrase she would like to say for her breath prayer, she thought for a moment, then said, "There's not a spot where God is not."

So that became Kelsie's breath prayer. Sometimes we would say it together, sometimes I would hear her whispering it when she was feeling sick or low. Eventually we ran out of curative treatments for Kelsie, and she went home to Montana, where she died surrounded by her loving parents.

Children may feel spiritual pain or suffering when they don't feel safe, or loved, or even attractive. A thirteen-year-old girl, whom I'll call Maddie, was diagnosed with a kind of bone cancer that resulted in her left leg being amputated below the knee. The medical team and the girl's parents had spent weeks discussing and preparing her for the amputation. We gave her and her family books, articles, web sites and education on what it would be like to live without a leg. We provided information on many different types of prosthetics and connected her with others her age who had lost a leg. For my part, I mostly listened and was present to her heartache and grief as she processed this enormous loss.

Maddie's mother was usually unwavering in her ability to allow her daughter to process and vent and rage and cry through her pain and grief over losing her leg. But parents are also grieving and struggling to come to terms with the reality that their child's life will be forever changed in a way this mother couldn't have begun to imagine just a few weeks ago. Sometimes a mother can't help but say something to her child that, while assuaging the mother's sorrow, may invalidate the child's feelings. Shortly before the surgery, I heard Maddie say to her mother, "I'll never get to see my leg—to see what it would have looked like *grown up*—whether it would have been pretty or ugly." Her mom thought for a moment, then replied, "Yes, but sweetie, if amputating that leg saves your life—it will be the most beautiful leg ever!" Though the response by Maddie's mother could be interpreted as glib or unmindful of Maddie's feelings, Maddie told me after her mother stepped out of the room, "I know she doesn't want me to die, and that's a good feeling." It was humbling to witness Maddie not only navigating her own pain and grief but so graciously accommodating her mother's pain and grief as well.

In addition to helping the patients themselves on their journey through spiritual pain, chaplains also do what we can to help their sisters and brothers. One day I was holding six-year-old Tory by the bed of her dying eight-year-old sister. Their mother was afraid Tory didn't understand that her sister was going away forever. From my arms, Tory leaned down and gave her sister a kiss. As she turned back into my arms, she whispered in my ear, "I'm going to miss her when she goes to heaven." So we talked about holding Tory's sister in what Tory called "Big Love," and then Tory gave her favorite teddy bear to her sister to comfort her on her journey. I think Tory understood her sister's journey quite well.

I am often asked whether siblings of children who are ill or dying should be made aware of the gravity of the situation. In my experience, children often know more than we think they do, and they are able to grasp even concepts as difficult as death better than we think they can. If you sit with a child and explain their own illness or a sibling's to them, they take in as much as they can at the time. It's important to remain open and available to them, knowing that they can and will ask questions over time (and sometimes not at the easiest of times!). I encourage parents to be honest and authentic with their children, sharing their own feelings and emotions appropriately. This not only helps children feel included but shows them that Mommy and Daddy are okay even though they are sad.

When people find out I am a chaplain at a children's hospital, they often ask how one provides spiritual care to children, because they assume children are too young to have formed any sense of spirit or of the sacred. Children, however, are the most spiritual beings I know. They make meaning of their lives and find hope in astounding ways. Like little Buddhas, they live in the present, so much so that they are a constant source of inspiration for me. When they are feeling good, it's a good day, and the most important thing to them at that time is the fruit roll-up. Why spoil it with worrying about how they may feel tomorrow?

The Unitarian Universalist approach to discussing spirituality with children involves listening to and wondering alongside them as they explore and discover their own approach to life experiences. I find at the hospital that their thinking is often unrestricted by dogma or doctrine, and it is up to each of us adults to hear where their hearts are leading them, whether that be toward a god or a particular religion or simply into the protective arms of their family and friends. Sophia Lyon Fahs wrote in *Today's Children and Yesterday's Heritage,* "One of the tragic ironies of history is that such original and creative geniuses as Buddha and Jesus have been extolled as perfect patterns for all to emulate. In the very struggle to be like someone else rather than to be one's own true self, or to do one's own best in one's own environment, a child is in danger of losing the pearl that is really beyond price—the integrity of his (or her) own soul."

Unlike adults, children have come so recently into existence "across the veil," or through the Light. I'm reminded of the mystic George MacDonald's verse:

Where have you come from, baby dear?

Out of everywhere, into here.

How can we come from "everywhere" and not bring some of the mystery, some of the Light, with us? A beautiful legend asserts that when a baby brushes her ear, an angel is whispering to her, "Don't forget . . . don't forget." Don't forget that place of deep love and warmth and comfort that you came from. And children don't forget—at least for a while. Without asking them, "What is your faith?" I can explore how they make meaning by asking questions like "What makes you feel safe? In whom or what do you trust? Who or what helps you when you need it? What brings you joy or makes you happy?"

Sometimes, having developed no shame or guilt for believing in something others may not understand, the children tell me about their spirituality without any prompting from me at all. One mother introduced me to her six-year-old daughter as "someone who talks about God." (This is not a way I would choose to be introduced, but the mother preempted my self-introduction.) Without missing a beat, her daughter replied, "Oh, I know all about God—she comes to visit me and sits on my bed at night when I'm scared. She has really pretty hair!" This child's mom looked shocked and said, "I have no idea where she got that—we've never even talked about God!" Then she suddenly turned to her daughter and asked, "God is a *woman?*" The little girl replied, "Oh, Mom!" shaking her head as if to say her mother really should know better.

It is vitally important that we as chaplains meet people—both adults and children—where they are spiritually and emotionally, striving to have no agenda of our own. In fact, professional certification requires that chaplains neither proselytize nor convert, and we may talk to patients about our own faith only with great discretion. My Unitarian Universalist faith not only supports my need to be open to, respectful of, and compassionately curious about the spiritual journeys and needs of others, it continuously challenges me to strengthen and broaden my notion of what it means to be open-hearted. Because my faith tradition is grounded in the principle of "the inherent worth and dignity of every person," I am emboldened and even inspired to meet people as they are, without judging their beliefs or their own faith traditions. As a Unitarian Universalist, I have been encouraged and even challenged to walk my own spiritual journey, which in turn has given me the ability to walk with others, whether Muslims or Jews or fundamentalist Christians. For providing spiritual care is about companioning patients and their families as they turn to what they need at the time they need it most.

On any given day, a mind-numbing number of patients at Children's Hospital are undergoing heart surgery, kidney transplants, chemotherapy, bone marrow transplants, and other drastic treatments. And a child's illness seems so much more painful, complex, and heart-wrenching than an adult's. For the children—our children—are truly our hope and our future. Yet I have seen parents find hope in the most difficult places. I have seen that, for our children, hope never dies, even when parents need to make a decision no parent should ever have to make.

A six-month-old boy, Levi, had been born with so many "anomalies" that his heart had difficulty beating and he had trouble breathing. He had spent all his short life at Children's Hospital. However, his parents' first son, Levi's four-year-old brother, had also been quite ill the first year of his life and was now an active, completely healthy boy. So Levi's parents were not about to give up on Levi. Even after several conferences with doctors who shook their heads and told the parents that continued care was futile, they insisted that everything possible be done for him.

Eventually, the medical staff began to feel that Levi's parents were not facing reality, so I was asked to spend more time with them. In visiting with them, I learned that they fully understood Levi's condition. They said, "We know that Levi could die or he could make it. You can't expect us to give up our hope, can you? It's what keeps him *and* us going!"

Whether I agreed with Levi's parents or the medical team didn't matter. What mattered was that I could be present with the parents and listen as they talked about the hopes and dreams they had had for Levi before he was discovered to be so ill. And I could be present with the team to allow them the space and time they needed to discuss their feelings and their frustration. I knew I was not going to take away the hope Levi's parents held on to. And I knew that Levi would probably not survive. But by standing with both the team, and then with the parents, I gave them each the opportunity to have their say and express their feelings. Doing so provided a little more space for all involved to take a breath and for Levi's parents to see that his body was not going to hold up to much more.

Two days later, Levi took a turn for the worse, and his parents agreed to withdraw life support. But before that happened, they wanted to take him outside. He had never been out under the sky or felt the wind on his face. So the Intensive Care Unit staff disconnected his mechanical ventilator and manually ventilated him as his mother carried him up to a patio on the roof of the hospital. And there, surrounded by more than a dozen family members and almost as many staff members, Levi took his last breath in the cool breeze of the early evening.

In the end, Levi's parents never stopped hoping. However, as his body struggled more and more to stay alive, their hope began to shift. The day before they decided to withdraw life support, I heard both parents move from saying, "He's a fighter! We know he can beat this!" to "We just don't want to see him suffer" and "We think he's getting tired." In the final hours of his life, they hoped that he could have a peaceful and pain-free death. They made this shift themselves and in their own time. Though I provided them with a caring presence and the space to share their heartbreak and devastation, they themselves, along with the medical team, came to what was best for Levi.

There is a lot to learn about hope not only from parents but from our patients as well. One seventeen-year-old young woman had struggled mightily with her diagnosis of aggressive cancer, and I met with her every time she came to the hospital, helping her practice meditation and mindfulness techniques to lessen her anxiety. When the medical team told her she had only months to live, I thought her despair would override any enjoyment she might be able to have at the end of her life. Instead she called me to tell me she had had beautiful wings tattooed across her shoulders. She told me, "This is my hope: that these wings take me where I need to go."

I am also reminded of Juan, sixteen years old, who died a couple years ago. At fourteen, he had walked and hitched rides from Guatemala to Seattle in order to live with his brother, work as a day laborer, and send money home to his mother, who had a heart condition and could not work. A year after he got to Seattle, his leg started to hurt and he was diagnosed with bone cancer. But every day, he would smile and laugh, attributing his good mood and his incredibly charming personality to God and to hope. He would say, in the little English that he knew, "Hope—it make happiness for me, yes!" These children are wise well beyond their years, and it is a gift to sit at their feet and learn from them every day. With great patience and generosity, they teach every one of us about life, death, and never-ending hope.

Hope, and companioning people as they find or retain their hope, does not mean taking away the pain or minimizing it in any way. Even if I could take away the pain, I shouldn't want to. For our pain and our losses are woven into the tapestry of our life. If I were to take away your pain, I would be robbing you of an experience that will profoundly affect your life. A missed stitch here, a flaw there, these make us who we are. There are many painful things in my life I would give anything to reverse. But I know that those painful times have made me the person— and the chaplain—that I am now. I won't be glib and tell you that pain and loss are gifts. But I do know that they change us and shape who we become.

At Children's Hospital, chaplains and other staff care for not just the bodies of our patients but also their hearts and their souls. I try to have no agenda when I walk into a patient's room. I'm familiar with different modalities of therapy, but as I work with those who are struggling to accept change, loss, or death, I am grounded in the knowledge that I am not there to fix, solve, advise, or assuage. I try to be a companion on their journey and to provide or be present to an awareness of feelings, of true nature, and of the Holy working in what Rita Nakashima Brock calls "the messy middle of our lives." This may mean that I leave a room with everyone feeling as devastated as when I walked in. Or it may mean that my presence has simply reminded a patient that they are not alone.

As I hold another's story in the vessel of my heart, I am called to give voice to right relation: to name that which obsesses or hooks us and causes us to spin on an axis of fear, woundedness, or simple unknowing. Mine is a ministry of attending and listening, what the theologian Nelle Morton calls "hearing people to speech" by offering them safety, honesty, an open heart, and at times a "soft place to fall." In this way, I hope to honor and lift up their connection to the sacred, to themselves, and to that which supports them and gives them the will to live into another day.

As I listen with empathy, it's not difficult for me to put myself in another's situation and imagine or intuit some of their feelings. But I know not to say, "I know just what you're going through," because, in truth, I don't know. I cannot know, because I am not them and have not been shaped by their family system or environment. I think of myself as having one foot in the circle and one foot out of it. The family is in the circle of grief and pain, and my own experiences of grief enable me to have one foot in it with them, empathizing with their loss and desolation. But I also have one foot firmly anchored outside the circle, partly because I'm not them and I don't know exactly how they feel, and partly because I have made it through difficult times myself and know it's possible that others will, too. And by having one foot out of the circle, I can better walk with the family through their darkness, because I don't become lost in their darkness or in my own difficulties with grief and loss. I am able to be that non-anxious presence who knows that somehow they will make it through. Their lives will be forever changed, but daylight will come.

As a chaplain, as a provider of spiritual care, I cannot fix a broken body or even heal an injured soul; but as a Unitarian Universalist who is called to this vocation, I can stand on the side of love and hope as I companion families through struggle and triumph. My days at the hospital are colored with conversation and silence, sadness and relief, loss and gratitude, loneliness and companioning, one foot in the circle and one foot out—suffering, faith, and hope. I dearly love it all.

I'll share one last story, to end with a little joy and even a little hope. Benny was a four-year-old with leukemia. His parents were pagan, and Benny had a strong and lively imagination. One day I was sitting with him while his mom was out taking a break. We were "fishing" using two crayons as fishing poles, with a piece of yarn tied to the end of each. On the other end of the yarn, I had tied a couple of paper clips as the hooks. When we first threw our hooks in the make-believe pond, Benny caught a fish right away. I said, "Oh, Benny, that's a *big* one!" "No, Kawen," he corrected me—he had a slight speech impediment—"it's willy *not* so big." Then I caught a fish, or thought I had, but Benny told me that, no, I had only gotten some weeds on my hook. Eventually, however, we had both caught several fish. I pointed to the make-believe pile of fish on the bed and asked Benny, "What are we going to do with all these fish?" He replied, "Cook 'em, Kawen." I asked, "What are we going to cook them in?" He thought for a moment, then reached behind himself and showed me an invisible item in his hand, saying, "In my invisible fwying pan that I keep in my invisible backpack!"

I learned that Benny kept all sorts of things in his invisible backpack—invisible snacks, toys, and his special friend, whom he had named "Hopeful." His mother told me that Benny brings out Hopeful whenever he's in pain or is sad. In my days at the hospital, I pray and hope that all the children, families, and staff members—that all of us—have in our invisible backpacks whatever we may need to see us through, including—especially including—a special friend named Hopeful.

Tending the Soul's Bones

KEITH W. GOHEEN

Do not be conformed to this world, but be transformed by the renewing of your minds, so that you may discern what is the will of God—what is good and acceptable and perfect.

—Romans 12:2

At the patient's bedside this morning, the team ended its rounds immersed in grim clouds of resignation. The clouds had first crept over the horizon several days ago. We saw them coming, as plainly as the Nor'easters that roar up the coast, but back then we had hope and time to skillfully beat back the darkness. Now the time and the hope were gone. Medicine would not prevail. Every reporting discipline shared its perspective. We had consensus, and we had no options. The storm was upon us. There was no port of refuge. We could only stand in the full force of the truth and change the goal of care.

As the team dispersed, the attending physician stopped at my shoulder. With a voice wearied by fatigue and defeat, he said, "Do what you can for the family. They deserved a better outcome." It was the referral I knew was coming. It was the referral I did not want. It is a referral for which I am prepared, to a task I am professionally trained to complete. "I will give them my best," I replied, and "Thank you." It was a very dense thank you, expressing appreciation for his confidence in me, reiterating the team's core values, and honoring the work, the worry, and the grief.

I practice a nonmedical specialty within a team of medical specialists. In the language of clinical medicine, my expertise is in spiritual care and I give special focus to the humanitarian goals of comfort and compassion in support of emotional and spiritual resilience. As a Unitarian Universalist minister, I feel called to this work, and as a board-certified chaplain, I am trained for it. This pairing of vocation and practice is a happy one. I work in a highly professional setting where I enter into the stories of others, journeying with them to places where the emotional and spiritual energies are often intense and at times transforming, and I learn from these experiences through an ongoing discipline of theological reflection.

This morning, in the room with large windows framing the quaint beauty of a seaside town, the professional consensus was that further curative treatment would be futile, and the focus of care made a radical shift. Unable to delay the patient's encounter with the inevitable fate of all humans, the team now made her comfort their primary goal. Emotions that had until now been held strategically in hopeful abeyance, especially by her family, were to be given a new freedom.

The team's decision to transition to comfort care heralded a radical shift in relationships. Everyone's future was now irrevocably changed, particularly the patient's and her family's. The once familiar structure of family life was about to undergo a powerful reordering. The family were brought into the room. The physician and the attending nurse faced them honestly, expressing loss and regret as they explained the new prognosis and plan of care. The howling winds of grief rushed into the space.

Amid the swirl of feelings, disorientation followed. Caught in storms of grief and despair, family members struggled to make sense of the words they were hearing. My fellow clinicians eased respectfully from the room, offering small comforts where they had once hoped to offer happy news. In their wake, I set to my task, beginning the work of mending the family's ruptured world by helping them find the meaning that would transmute the pain of loss into the wisdom of life.

Spiritual care centers on the human ability to make meaning from experience. Spirituality is always relational because the most human and humanizing aspect of our connectedness, spirituality, is embedded in every relationship. To recognize the spiritual character of the relationships within the families in my care, I must be well tuned to the spiritual character of my own professional and personal relationships. Until I can connect my humanity to others' humanity, I cannot offer spiritual care. The character and spiritual power of these relationships is stored in the stories I remember. I have learned to value these stories as guides and teachers. As a chaplain, I must also be a master of my stories, so that they inform my work without intruding into the families' stories, causing me to violate the principle of patient-centered care.

Standing just inside the door of the hospital room, I grow aware of old feelings and memories of loss and dying. I survey the room and make quick spiritual assessments. What stories are unfolding? The daughter moves to her mother's bedside and pours out her heart to her, as her husband rests his hands and head on his spouse's shoulders. Her father, the patient's husband, returns to the comforting cocoon of the reclining chair where he has logged many hours in quiet vigil, but the alertness of his posture is gone. He slumps, forlornly fixing his gaze on the floor. They are in spiritual distress, but it is the young adult son, standing rigid, alone in the corner with his back to the wall, who seems most deeply in the throes of an internal struggle. He is in spiritual crisis and most at risk of trauma.

I remember the stories of other sons and gather the energy of those memories into my body. Moving toward him, I bring this energy as a spiritual gift, a healing balm distilled from the experiences of those who have made this journey before him. As I move deeper into the space, listening, affirming, and comforting as one human soul to another, the force of the tempest begins to subtly change. Within the hour, the feeling in the room will be very different. The healing will have begun.

As a chaplain, I find it helpful to imagine the family as a body, with a skeletal soul fleshed out with personality. Each family member is a part of the larger whole and contains the essence of the whole. When I speak of a family body, I am talking about an intangible yet organic body animated by a network of intimate emotional and spiritual relationships. It is through the shared energy of these relationships that the body's members create important identity roles. These roles give external form to their inner emotional lives. The family is also an essential place for the development of human character, the means by which people embody life's transcending purposes and meanings. Role identity is shaped by personality, principally concerned with survival, and under the care of the ego. Character rises out of the soul and incarnates the nature of the human spirit, which is concerned with generativity and fulfillment. (My thinking here draws on the Jungian concept of the soul, as discussed by James Hillman in *The Force of Character and the Lasting Life.*)

Spiritually healthy people are comfortable in their roles and flexible in their functioning as the stresses of life press upon the family body. They are able to stay true to themselves. Their stories vary widely and will be touched with a colorful range of emotions. When their sense of who they are and what family means is threatened, individuals and their families feel stress and become less flexible. Preservation of the family narrative becomes more important, and they focus on a narrower set of stories emphasizing survival and on the values that centrally shape their identity, while limiting the stories' emotional content. Simply being in the hospital can activate stress responses ranging from mild to pronounced. For those in spiritual distress, the chaplain can be a calming, centering presence, helping restore generativity to the stressed relationships. A non-anxious presence helps emotional flexibility return and problem solving replace stubborn resistance.

If the threat is sufficiently strong, it can trigger a spiritual crisis, a spiritual state wherein the relationships that have provided core identity roles and their accompanying meanings are no longer dependable and may even seem wholly absent. Stories that were once shared lose their meaning and their orienting power, causing a profound loss of identity, purpose, and sense of connection. Individuals and families in spiritual crisis are often either emotionally numb or fiercely angry; they have lost their ability to adapt to change and with it the capacity to express grief. They need an external relationship that they trust enough to allow it to support them as they explore new ways of being in relationship and create new meaning in their new and dramatically altered roles. Only then can they mourn their losses and safely reenter their overarching life story.

Kevin, the son who stands mute and rigid in his mother's hospital room, appears fragile despite his muscular frame. He is in spiritual crisis. From earlier visits, I know that Kevin's identity is still closely bound to his parents and dependent on their physical presence. He is frightened more than sorrowful and needs the support of another person with whom he can find and share his fear. Because he sees the loss of his mother's physical presence as a total loss of the relationship, a spiritual as well as a physical death, his spiritual bones are at risk of snapping under the weight of this loss. Kevin is not mustering the spiritual resources to transform his spiritual connection with his mother, anchoring it not in physical presence but in memory. He will need his family for this work, but in this moment they are deeply immersed in the labors of their individual souls. So I step in, drawing on the role he and I share of loving son, offering refuge in a common identity and quietly lending him a pastoral presence deeply rooted in the larger, transcending story of life. His shallow, panicky breathing deepens. Still wordless but growing teary-eyed, Kevin begins to feel safe enough to accept his grief. The most immediate danger is passing. I begin to move among the others, sharing a word, a touch, while honoring the prayerful silence, the fear and the awe.

Among the others, I find healthy levels of spiritual distress. Frank, the husband slumping in the hospital recliner, is deep in his grief, but it is not challenging his sense of self. He is a practical man who has already buried his parents and two siblings, and his spiritual skeleton is sufficiently formed to carry the fleshy weight of his loss. Daughter Leeann's words and tears mingle in a stream of grief. She has created a life outside the protective circle of her parents' home, and so her spiritual skeleton is strong enough to hold the moment. The physical support of her husband, Randy, combines with the spiritual strength growing in their relationship to bolster Leeann's resources as she negotiates with her ego and discovers the spiritual strength of character to renegotiate her covenant with her mother. Freeing her mother from the obligation of physical presence, an obligation that had already diminished with Leann's transition to adult independence, helps Leeann begin to rely on the spiritual power of their relationship, which will remain vibrant in memory. Their love will transcend death.

In time, the whirlwinds of private grief begin to abate. Family members begin to look around for each other. First with eye contact, then words, and finally with physical movement, they come together for the first time as a family in the midst of transformation. The emotional intensity of their spiritual distress eases. The family skeleton, battered by death's body blows, begins the long, hard work required to reconstitute a new wholeness, a wholeness that holds the possibility of a stronger family character.

The dynamic relationships between soul and ego, world and God, form the axial relationships energizing the spiritual life. Their stability and centrality are profoundly challenged in crisis. Ego strength, drawing its energy from the immediate situation, is molded by adaptive behaviors learned over time. Ego strength is adequate for daily living, but it cannot withstand the permanence of death because death is antithetical to the ego's primary function, the drive for preservation. We can use ego energy to rearrange the structure of our lives and adapt to many changes, but it is not sufficient to power the work of transformation, the essential work of death and dying.

Death is what makes us human. Only death has the power to release the fullness of character harbored in the human soul. Every death we experience, whether it is a physical death, the death of the sense of invulnerability that comes with a glimpse into our own mortality, or the death of a hope, an idea, or a belief, causes the ego to retract, opening a space within human consciousness for the soul to expand.

As the soul expands and character emerges, we gain spiritual maturity and, with it, the corresponding generativity that we celebrate in the lives of our saints and martyrs. Spiritual maturity is evidenced in emotional autonomy. It allows the person to become more present in the world and less defined by it. Spiritual maturity's poise and creativity are sustained by the strength of character flowing to us from the enduring strength of God's generativity, coming into the human life by way of the soul. A well-grounded spiritual life is essential in professional chaplaincy. The knowledge and personality which serve us admirably in the day-to-day world cannot sustain the continuing demands inherent in the work of caring for people in spiritual distress and crisis. Spiritual generativity requires me to faithfully attend to my relationship with the transcending reality that is God. Neglecting this spiritual relationship puts both me and the patient in spiritual danger, because then we both may lack sufficient emotional energy to respond effectively to the crisis at hand. Kevin and his family were safe in my spiritual care because, like the other clinicians with whom I serve, I practice and develop the skills and arts of a generative spiritual practice. But what of Roseanne, the woman in the hospital bed? She is entirely dependent on life support, unresponsive to external stimuli, so thoroughly debilitated that, despite the intrusive treatments, she requires no sedation to keep her quiet. By the usual standards, Rosanne is beyond participating in our relationships. Voice and touch might still stir responses in her, and her family conduct themselves with the assumption that she is "still here." Is she already just a memory whose physical shadow still lingers on the hospital bed, or are the familial relationships in touch with a larger reality?

If Roseanne is her personality, then she is "gone." No cognitive function means no ego function, and thus she has lost her personality. But her character and her soul are more difficult to observe. If the soul is intimately connected to God and is not dependent on the mind's cognitive abilities, then it has its being independent of the mind and offers an alternative form of consciousness. If the soul expands into the void left by the retreating ego, then it seems likely that these already dramatic hours may find Roseanne fully attuned to the presence of God. It is also reasonable to assume that she remains aware of the spiritual dimension of her relationships with her family and with the chaplain and other caregivers.

We are limited in our ability to be consciously present to this in-pouring of spiritual riches, but if holy mystics such as Mechthild of Magdeburg and Meister Eckhart are right in saying that the release of the ego bond brings an ecstatic union with the Divine, then the serenity that comes over the faces of the dying may be real, not merely imagined by anguished families watching their loved one's facial muscles relax and yield up the tensions of life. Having observed many families grow more comfortable as the patient's presence wanes, I agree with the faith that proclaims a transcending love. I am with the mystics. There is good news, even in death. Peace with God is real. The transcending story is true.

Old as death, the transcending story is the spiritual story and the story of the one transcending life that gives rise to all other lives. Human spirituality is that part of the life force of God that has entered the human experience. We experience it as the soul-deep, creative passion to realize the relational potentials in each emerging moment.

In the hours of transition as Roseanne lay dying, her family and I participated in a powerfully human transformation. Relational forms that had long existed were also dying. The spiritual bones of those relationships were dissolving, relinquishing the last energies of their potential. In their place, another new and tender set of relational ties were beginning to grow. Saturated with generative possibilities, these emerging relationships would support the physical, emotional, and spiritual restructuring of the family's internal and external worlds.

These transformations of the family also inform and subtly alter God's being. As the people in the hospital room are realizing the potential for new, meaning-filled ways of being in relationship, so too is God. They share their experiences of Roseanne's death through the mediating relationship of their souls. The experience of human death is vital to God because God cannot have direct knowledge of this one experience. In this (as Charles Hartshorne suggests in *A Natural Theology for Our Time* and *The Divine Relativity: A Social Conception of God*), God is in need of humanity and the rest of the temporal world.

Through a relationship with human souls, God experiences

creativity's destructive power, the human reality of death. As Roseanne's soul moves into ecstatic union with God, God gains a more intimate knowledge of death. She surrenders into eternity and God tastes finitude. This profoundly experiential sharing between souls is the heart of the divine covenant. Standing quietly around the bed, witnessing the terrible loss and the beautiful gifts moving in this now sacred space, we are attending to the ongoing fulfillment and renewal of God's covenant with God's people.

Beyond the windows, the low-hanging sun throws dark, bony fingers across the town and its inhabitants. Roseanne's body has been still for several minutes. The emotional storm has spent its energy. A silent resonance fills the space. My chest begins to feel lighter, as if my breath is returning. Almost imperceptibly, a restlessness begins to stir among the survivors.

"I guess it's over," says Kevin. I nod in affirmation and note the reverent tone in his voice. For a moment, the silence returns. Then Frank announces, "She's not in pain anymore." At the sound of her father's words, Leeann's tears return. She gazes intently into her mother's face: "I miss you so much, Mom." Like a soul shaking off the dream sleep of mortality, conversation awakens, and the family reassembles away from the bed. Fear and assurance ebb and flow in their words and faces. As we drift slowly and uncertainly toward the door, the talk turns to faith. "She is at peace." "She is in heaven with Charlie and Minnie." "And Aunt Clara." "I know she will be watching over us."

Dense with feeling and meaning, their words express appreciation for Roseanne's life, reminding each person of the core spiritual bonds that give their lives value and honoring their work, their worry, and their grief. Their faith is affirmed. Roseanne, like all who have gone before her, is safely enfolded into the life of God. They know this because they have found a new, if fragile, sense of wholeness. As it is in heaven, so shall it be on Earth.

As the family moves down the hall, sharing goodbye hugs with caregivers and receding from my view, I pull the curtain around Roseanne's bed and stand for a moment amid the prayerful silence. Then I move to the nurse's station and make

a final entry in the patient's chart: "Provided pastoral support
and prayer to family at time of patient's death. Family is in deep
mourning but coping effectively. They plan to utilize personal
grief support resources. Family expressed gratitude for the care
provided by staff." In a few hours, the pager will sound again,
and the never-ending journey will begin anew.

From the time the chaplain first enters the unit until the last
chart note is entered, assessment is essential to effective spiritual care. The chaplain needs to continue the assessing process
throughout because the patient is impacted by changes anywhere in the relational support system. Understanding how the
patient is currently engaging in relationships allows the chaplain to get a clearer picture of the patient's spiritual resources
and deficits as they emerge. Relationships can be mapped easily,
but their relative value to the patient may vary from moment to
moment as the patient's perceptions are reformed by conscious
and unconscious processes and by the changing availability and
perceptions of the people around them.

Amid this flowing river of information, the chaplain attempts
to tap into the appropriate spiritual current. The most effective way of assessing relational value and perception is to listen
to the stories. Stories manifest relational values, which in turn
are manifestations of the spiritual life. Assessing the structure,
themes, and momentum of stories provides critical insights into
the relational support system's health and with it the patient's
spiritual well-being. Stories should be analyzed in multiple
ways, and having an assortment of assessment tools enriches
the chaplain's ability to intervene skillfully.

One assessment tool I use with great frequency examines
the roles taken by members of the relational body. Understanding the roles participants play allows the chaplain to assess and
intervene in the story's movement. Roles are centers of spe-
cialized authority, particular identities that individuals focus
on allowing the spiritual work and emotional responsibility to
be distributed. Participants cannot always identify their roles
in particular situations, because roles are assigned through an
often unconscious process based on a collective vision derived
from cultural history. The chaplain specializes in the work

involved in discovering, naming, and supporting the family's relational matrix, along with the underlying spiritual resources that empower the matrix and give it its meaning. This work is especially important when the matrix interferes with the medical staff's ability to provide care or when the family's needs exceed what the staff can offer.

I have developed the Spiritual Roles tool as a way to obtain a quick, comprehensive, and systematic assessment of the relational body's connections. Like an X-ray, it reveals the spiritual bones that support the story. The tool is based on Peter Tuft Richardson's work utilizing dimensions of the Myers-Briggs Type Indicator (MBTI) personality inventory (as described in his book, *Four Spiritualities*) and grounded in the pioneering work of the psychoanalyst Carl Jung. Richardson identifies four primary spiritual journeys: Unity, Harmony, Devotion, and Works. Because these journeys are imbued with distinct perspectives and expectations, the people on them prefer to do their spiritual work in different ways, and these preferences contribute to the formation of roles. Recognizing these roles allows the chaplain to identify the underlying spiritual resources from which each participant draws strength and inspiration.

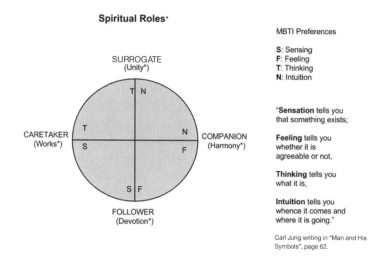

Spiritual Roles*

MBTI Preferences

S: Sensing
F: Feeling
T: Thinking
N: Intuition

SURROGATE
(Unity*)

T N

CARETAKER
(Works*)

T
S

N
F

COMPANION
(Harmony*)

S F

FOLLOWER
(Devotion*)

"**Sensation** tells you
that something exists;

Feeling tells you
whether it is
agreeable or not,

Thinking tells you
what it is,

Intuition tells you
whence it comes and
where it is going."

Carl Jung writing in "Man and His
Symbols", page 62.

In this mandala, each of the four roles is placed in relationship to one another based on shared personality traits. Every person can assume any one of the roles, though everyone has a preferred, personality-based, relational role. Depending on the changing needs of the family, individuals may change roles. It is easier to shift roles along the circle: for instance, moving from Follower to Caretaker, than it is to move across the radius: moving from Caretaker to Companion. The Follower and Caretaker share a preference for Sensing, while the Caretaker and Companion share no preferences.

Taken as a whole, the circle represents the potential for spiritual wholeness within the family. Knowing where key family members stand on the circle and how ably they can fill the role helps the chaplain to identify the family's overall spiritual health and to identify the places where roles may be ill-fitting, absent, weak, or overpowering, unbalancing the circle and causing spiritual distress or crisis.

The four cardinal roles are:

- **SURROGATE** (Unity): The Surrogate speaks with the authority of the patient. Compassionately in tune with them, the Surrogate is confident, speaking for them in making choices and evolving meaning out of changing circumstances.

- **COMPANION** (Harmony): The Companion stands in intimate relationship with the patient but maintains a perspective from beside them. The Companion is willing to speculate about the patient's wishes and understands the values and meanings they would use, but does not advocate. Instead, the Companion shares insights into the patient's desires by remembering where the Companion's values and meanings are similar to and different from those of the patient.

- **FOLLOWER** (Devotion): The Follower looks to the patient as a leader, mentor, or parent figure. A close student of the patient, the Follower knows their heart and mind but avoids anticipating their choices or the new meaning emerging from the situation.

- CARETAKER (Works): Often focused on physical symptoms and treatment, the Caretaker finds purpose in providing for the patient's identified needs. The Caretaker may have the most difficulty discerning choices in complex and ambiguous circumstances, especially if the decisions are to be based on abstract values like quality of life.

Each role tends to prefer the modes of gathering and processing information that adjoin it, so that the role a person is playing may be identified by the modes they use to function in the larger system. It is relatively easy for a person to move from one role to another that is adjacent to it on the circumference of the circle, because the two roles share a mode. Axial roles, across the circle from each other, are complementary in that together they utilize all four modes; but because they have opposite preferences, one is usually more strongly developed than the other within an individual psyche, and it is more difficult to move along an axis than around the circumference. The health of each role affects the functioning of each of the others, in both internal and external relational systems.

Individually and collectively, people take on all four of these roles in their lives, emphasizing one or another according to the situation. An individual must have a basic level of competence in each in order to be functionally healthy. Falling below basic competence gives rise to spiritual distress and can, in radically changing relationships, precipitate a spiritual crisis.

Roles may be tightly defined, readily shared, or exchanged in accordance with the underlying relational agreements and abilities of the relational body's constituents. In the hospital, the Caretaker role is always reserved for the staff as defined through the patient/physician relationship, but anyone may participate in another role. Chaplains, or other key caregivers, may need to fill in absent or underdeveloped roles for families in crisis, temporarily entering their circle of relationships to provide balance and allow the relational body to begin restoring its natural order.

Looking back at the unfolding story in Roseanne's room on that day of profound transitions, I can use the Spiritual Roles tool diagnostically, gaining insights into ways that the family was coping effectively and identifying the point of crisis that would require skilled intervention.

Throughout the preceding week, Frank had been at his wife's bedside in much the same way that he had always been in relationship with her. Theirs had been a highly collaborative household, in which they shared duties, worries, and joys as a couple. They were companions. While the responsibility for Roseanne's care decisions had settled heavily onto Frank's shoulders, he accepted the weight in the spirit of partnership. In Frank's words, "She would do this for me. The least I can do is accept the truth and do this for her." He was able to make critical decisions from the perspective of the Companion, indicating that the spiritual dimension of their marriage was intact and providing the values necessary for him to grasp the meaning and fulfill his role.

Leeann remained the devoted daughter, the Follower. While the parting was intensely painful for her, she was able to imagine new ways to remain loyal to her mother. She spoke of continuing love and promised that she would "look after daddy," in imitation of her mother's care for her father. Leeann also followed her mother's example in her own relationship with her husband, Randy, as they shared the experience of Roseanne's hospitalization and now her death. The severity of her loss is likely to be ameliorated in time as she incorporates this new way of being in the world into her daily life.

Struck dumb by terror and unable to express his grief and fear, Kevin was at risk of spiritual crisis. He identified very closely with his mother, but he could not be her Surrogate. He was too deep in crisis to advocate for himself. Immature in his identity as an adult child and with his personality still developing, Kevin lacked the internal organization to support the emotional autonomy essential to the healthy internal expression of the Surrogate role. Additionally, taking on the Surrogate or Caretaker role with his mother would have put him in competition with his father, from whom he still needed much emotional support. He was, in effect, emotionally and spiritually dismembered, unable to connect with the people he needed the most. The family body would best support Kevin in the role of Follower, where he could safely form a partnership with his sister and share in the work of mourning. An opening had to be made in the membrane of fear smothering Kevin's soul so that his spirit could be reunited with the life-giving energy of the relational body.

As a chaplain, I sensed that the greatest barrier to Kevin making this transition was his inability to express the overwhelming feelings roiling inside him, causing his relational paralysis. Because he was unable to gain perspective on his inner life, I offered to establish a relationship in which we were Companions. With supportive words and body language, I sought to mirror his inner state in the hope that he would recognize himself. Developing a relationship with a Companion allowed him to gain enough distance from his feelings to begin to name them, or to at least recognize their names when I spoke of feelings I had experienced. In this exchange, he gained some mastery and a desperately needed opening to reconnect. I knew that the intervention was successful when he began to move out of our shared space and toward his mother's bed—importantly, on the side occupied by his sister. With faltering steps, Kevin was able to move toward the role of bereaved Follower.

Roseanne's companionable leadership will be much missed. It is the spiritual character of the Follower that eventually reunites the family. The thoughts they share as they depart demonstrate a close harmony, indicating that the Companion role is still active, though in a secondary capacity, a healthy psychological buttress against crisis. They will remain in relationship and devoted to this woman and the values she will continue to represent, as they express them in their lives in the years ahead.

Jesus of Nazareth spoke often of the Kingdom of God. His metaphors pointed toward a coming age, but also suggested that it was, and had always been, already present. It was as if the

Kingdom was always here, but humanity could not notice it. I believe it was Jesus' aim to use parables as tools to awaken his audience, that they might be transformed in their new state of consciousness. As a hospital chaplain, I see the timeless and time-bound paradox embedded in the Gospel stories come into sharp relief as I witness patients, families, and staff finding new levels of relational meaning and spiritual wholeness already within and among themselves.

Jesus knew, as did all the great religious figures of history, that we carry in our bones the spiritual potential for wholeness, and we have the entirety of our lives to nurture this potential into reality. Precious few of us complete the task by walking all four of Richardson's spiritual journeys to their ends, but all of us can, through the spiritual discipline of relational covenants, contribute to our own and others' growth by sharing stories from our diverse journeys and allowing others to call us, as individuals and relational bodies, toward new stages of spiritual awareness. We have within us the likeness of God, and we have the means by which to explore it.

As a chaplain, a Unitarian Universalist minister, and a human being, I continue to discover spiritual value in the journeys of others, especially the individuals and families who travel paths different from mine and whose stories are populated with different characters, values, and meanings. By carefully attending to the multitude of cultural stories tangential to mine, I can see, at least dimly, the transcending spiritual story, ever present and ever accessible, awaiting fuller comprehension. I feel my professional and personal lives growing increasingly meaningful. Supported by the evidence derived from effective assessment tools, my intuition grows more authoritative. I appreciate the ways it chooses among our delightfully subtle palette of emotional colors to paint impressionistic portraits of the spiritual life. This growing body of evidence inspires my thinking in ways that compel me to see an ever more precise model of the beautifully complex relational universes within and among human souls. I am better able to comprehend these wondrous structures and become more adept at sharing the good news: Amid the pain and brokenness in the world and in our souls, our relationships have the power to heal.

Henry David Thoreau chose to live his life very intentionally. In *Walden*, he writes,

> I went to the woods because I wished to live deliberately, to front only the essential facts of life, and see if I could not learn what it had to teach, and not, when I came to die, discover that I had not lived. I did not wish to live what was not life, living is so dear; nor did I wish to practise resignation, unless it was quite necessary. I wanted to live deep and suck out all the marrow of life, to live so sturdily and Spartan-like as to put to rout all that was not life, to cut a broad swath and shave close, to drive life into a corner, and reduce it to its lowest terms, and, if it proved to be mean, why then to get the whole and genuine meanness of it, and publish its meanness to the world; or if it were sublime, to know it by experience, and be able to give a true account of it in my next excursion.

For me, Thoreau captures the investigative spirit behind evidence-based spiritual care. The tools I use today, and those I will acquire in the years ahead, will bring comfort and hope to those with whom I practice because they are the same instruments by which I examine and cultivate wholeness in my spiritual life.

We can do none of this work alone. Spirituality is the marrow inside the bones of our relationships. Maybe this need to be in relationship is why we—physicians, staff, patients, and families—are here. Called forward by an ultimate and enduring passion for life that cannot be silenced, we are pulled together into the care of astonishingly complex physical bodies that are both resilient and fragile. Ever mindful of death's encroaching shadow, we are also pulled together into an organic, spiritually amazing, relational body. The more precisely we understand the workings of the physical body, the more effectively we can utilize medicine to address its ills. The more vibrant and subtle our perceptions of the transcending story and the workings of the Spirit become, the more potently we can draw on our spirituality and heal the relational bodies essential to the well-being of the soul.

In hospital room after hospital room, the sick and the broken appear before us, a complicated admixture of health and disease, hope and despair, strength and helplessness. We offer them hospitality and join them in the struggle. The tasks may be at times routine, but they are never without consequence; to the patient, certainly, but in truth all of us bear the consequences of our relationships. We cannot, in good conscience, remain conformed to the world of our current understanding. All are transformed in the caring.

Wider Circles of Inclusion

HOLLY ANNE LUX-SULLIVAN

The woman standing in front of me is the granddaughter of my patient. She is a born-again Christian about my age who was initially friendly toward me but is beginning to allow her suspicion to show: "I saw the 'Coexist' bumper sticker on your car. What's *that* about?" "It's about respecting everyone's beliefs," I say.

She asks what it means, exactly, to be a hospice chaplain. I tell her it's about working with people wherever they are in their spiritual journey, whether they're Christians, atheists, or Buddhists. First she says her own faith wouldn't allow her to work as a chaplain because she would need to lead people to Jesus and tell them the Truth (you could hear the capital T). Then she looks at me and asks, without a hint of humor, "So what do you tell atheists—'Hell isn't *that* hot'?"

I pray that angry blood isn't rushing to my cheeks as I feel heat surging into my chest. I smile and let out a nervous giggle, then say, "No, I talk with them about what they want from the last weeks or months of their lives and how I can help them through this time."

The conversation veers, disturbingly, to her thoughts on homosexuality and abortion. She is not, shall we say, a proponent of marriage equality. These are the moments that are so hard for me: finding the balance between being true to what I believe so deeply and establishing or maintaining relationships with the people to whom I minister. I remind myself repeatedly: It's not about me or the many LGBT people I care about. It's about *her* life and experiences, past and present. The conversation feels like an attack on those I love, but it isn't. Still, I get the distinct impression she's testing me in some way.

To my surprise, her opposition to abortion comes from her own experience; she had one before she was born again. Now she talks with women like herself about the forgiveness God has to offer. Yes, for her abortion is the taking of a life, a sin, but it doesn't mean God doesn't still love her and all those women like her. Admittedly, I'm shocked—and delighted—by this turn. I'm reminded that even fundamentalist Christians can have layers and recognize nuance.

Still, I leave the patient's house angry in a way I know is far out of proportion: Her comment about her own inability to serve as a chaplain made me doubt my own faith. Ought I not be evangelizing for Unitarian Universalism? I let her intolerance make me doubt myself and my deep belief in religious tolerance, diversity, and inclusion. It was not my finest hour as a chaplain. I was busy worrying about whether I was visibly angry. I handled my discomfort as professionally as I could, but I wasn't a very good chaplain to her because I got in my own way. I let her make our interaction about me. When her grandmother died, she asked if a more traditional hospice chaplain was available to do the funeral—not me, because I was too "eclectic."

When I began my first internship as a hospital chaplain five years ago, I knew without a doubt that, because I am a Unitarian Universalist, I would be the most open-minded chaplain-in-training there. But it took just a few minutes of rounding on my unit to meet my first Southern Baptist patient and his family, to hear him declare, "As long as you believe in the Word, you're all right by me!" and to recognize how intolerant I truly was. It wasn't that I couldn't imagine believing in the Bible; rather, I was upset because I couldn't imagine believing in one and only one way, one and only one truth—for all people, for all time. More than that, I was shocked that he had stated it so bluntly, as though it were simple fact. Where I live, in a rural county in central North Carolina, it *is* simple fact, but I was more than a little ignorant of that at the time. Stunned into silence, I faced my own previously unrecognized prejudices and assumptions, about myself as well as about those I served and worked with.

My smugness going into chaplaincy showed me how far I had to come—and working as a chaplain now continues to show me how far I still have to go. It has also made me keenly aware of how much work many Unitarian Universalists have to do to truly accept Christians; all too often we seem to think that most if not all Christians are imbeciles. In the years between meeting my first unapologetic Southern Baptist and now, I have struggled to make peace with conservative Christian theology and to respect, and provide care for, its believers. That's involved everything from praying very Christian prayers to talking with a family about their desire to try to raise up their newly deceased loved one.

My co-workers in my first Clinical Pastoral Education group were a liberal Presbyterian and a conservative evangelical Christian. I dreaded the day my evangelical colleague would encounter a gay patient, fearing not only the things he would say to the rest of us about the person but also how he might treat them, perhaps berating him about his "lifestyle" being unnatural and sinful. Mind you, I never heard him say any such thing. I merely jumped to the conclusion that he would, on the basis of his church's stated beliefs.

The reality is that my conservative Christian colleague was able to minister to a young woman contemplating abortion not with judgment and fear-mongering but with love and compassion. I learned that's what Christian love is: A man seeing a young woman's pain and helping her address it rather than condemning her or calling her out as a sinner.

My life and ministry have been made immeasurably richer by my (admittedly compulsory) interactions with people whose faiths differ from my own, most notably conservative Christians. Some of them have shown me that the love of Jesus looks like a sister refusing to let her brother die alone despite his years of alcoholism and its attendant manipulation, deceit, and heartbreak. They have shown me, too, how challenging it is to believe in "the inherent worth and dignity of every person." And in the process they have made me a better Unitarian Universalist.

When I became a hospice chaplain, my chaplain colleagues and supervisor were aware that I'm a Unitarian Universalist, but the nurses and social workers I would work alongside every day hadn't seen my resume and credentials. Many of them have framed quotations from the Bible on their desks or little signs that say things like "God is good" and "Don't worry about tomorrow. God is already there."

Please understand, I was a journalist in my former life, which meant I was surrounded by happily godless heathens like myself—mostly transplanted Northerners, too—and the Christians among us were not the kind of Christians who put framed scripture on their desks. Or, if they would have liked to, they nonetheless didn't, because they suspected (rightly) that they'd be made fun of in our cynical, sarcastic newsroom.

So I experienced some fairly severe culture shock when I came to the hospice, because suddenly my co-workers— co-workers who *weren't* chaplains—talked about God. A lot. When they say they'll pray for someone, they aren't kidding. When we gather in a circle and pray around the one in need of prayer, they add words of gratitude for the freedom to pray at work.

And my little Unitarian Universalist self had to learn how to navigate this strange new world in which people who are not religious professionals talk about their faith regularly. Lucky for me, going to divinity school, doing an internship, and training as a hospital chaplain for almost three years cured me of all my issues with Christians, right?

Sadly, no. I had been in my position for three full months before I came out as a Unitarian Universalist to my team of nurses and social workers, and even then it was something of an accident. One day, when one of the social workers said something wonderfully hateful, I said, "You're going straight to hell! And I'm a *Universalist!*" wanting to emphasize that if even a Universalist thinks you're going to hell, you must have done something really bad, right?

But the joke was lost on my audience. For my colleagues who were born, raised, and educated firmly within the Bible Belt, my comment sparked questions about what Universalists are and what they believe. I gave my thirty-second history lesson: "Unitarians were heretics because they believed God was one and that Jesus was a prophet, not the actual son of God, and Universalists were heretics because they believed their loving God would not damn anyone to hell for all eternity, and fifty years ago all the heretics got together, and now we believe lots of different things."

One co-worker said incredulously, "So you don't believe in hell?" "No, I don't," I told her, "and most Unitarian Universalists would probably say the same thing." She asked what our doctrine is, and I said we're a nondoctrinal denomination.

I was certain this brief conversation would cause my co-workers' idea of me to change. They don't understand what Unitarian Universalism is. It's new and weird to them, to lots of people. I don't really understand conservative Christianity, either, though doctrinally speaking I get the gist.

What I don't understand is how loving, generous, compassionate people can believe in religious tenets that seem to me to be full of hate. And though I wish my colleagues were more accepting, I still know them to be loving, generous, compassionate people. I have seen them treat their co-workers, patients, and patients' families well regardless of their sexual orientation or religion. Yet I was afraid they wouldn't still see me as compassionate and loving, because I don't believe as they do.

I was asking them to do for me what I had been doing for them: getting to know someone and making judgments about them on the basis of personal knowledge of them rather than on what church they go to or what that church's website says its members believe. I'm glad to say my new co-workers didn't disappoint me. Nothing has been different or weird between us since my big coming out.

Around the time of my first anniversary at the hospice agency, I had a conversation with one of these conservative Christian co-worker friends about how I handle ministering to those who believe differently than I do. She was simply curious, but her curiosity led to a talk about our beliefs in which she revealed that my Mother Earth flag had been a bit of a tipoff that maybe I wasn't your standard-issue Christian chaplain. And here I thought I had been somewhat under-the-radar to start with! We laughed about it, and it felt like we got a little bit closer that day as a result.

The key for me has been not trying to tackle conservative Christianity as a whole, or as a concept, but to meet the people in front of me and see who they are. I've stopped looking up my new friends' churches online because I know the "beliefs" section of the website will upset me: It will define the Bible as the literal and inerrant word of God, Jesus Christ as the one path to salvation, and marriage as only between a man and a woman. That is what most of my co-workers believe, and I disagree wholeheartedly; but I also see how these co-workers treat their patients and colleagues, whatever their orientation and beliefs. I see the care and love they give their patients, some of whom are avowed atheists, some of whom are liberal Christians, and some of whom—very few, yes, but some—are even Hindu or Buddhist. My conservative co-workers don't proselytize to their patients. Instead, they ask me if there are particular customs they should follow but aren't familiar with, or things they should be sure not to do with a Buddhist, Hindu, or even Moravian Christian family. They want to learn and to do right by their patients, even if their faith tells them they should be proselytizing to any non-Christians they meet.

I also feel how they treat me and how they interact with me, their chaplain colleague, whose desk doesn't have a cross on it but does have a small collection of stones and a carved Buddha. They trust me with their own heartaches and difficulties, and though I find their faith hard to understand (as surely they do mine), we are able to connect because I'm not interacting with evangelical Christianity or the church they attend: I'm interacting with the person right in front of me.

Co-workers are usually relatively easy to get along with despite these kinds of differences. When the person in front of you is a member of our own family, things get exponentially more complicated. A parent, sibling, or cousin says something that rankles us, and the baggage from decades of relationships inevitably rears its head. There's no separating one offensive comment from years of fraught relationships. Every word feels like an attack.

The cliche "pick your battles" exists for moments like this: Your parent, in-law, or Aunt Jill is preaching to you over a holiday meal and you've all but bitten through your tongue. What now?

Well, ask yourself: How have similar conversations gone in the past? Is this family member someone who can engage in conversation about difference without being cruel or offensive? Can I?

We have to know what our emotional triggers are—topics and people—and if we can't handle a conversation reasonably, or if we know from experience that the other person can't, we need to remove ourselves from it. Be honest, especially about your own limitations. It's easy to put blame on the other person, but I know I'm at least as guilty of bad behavior as they are. Some of us can't keep our tempers with a particular family member no matter what we're talking about. We have to be honest with ourselves about what we're capable of. Sometimes we have to walk away, for the sake of family harmony and our own blood pressure. It's far better to let your family think you're rude for walking away from a conversation than to get into a shouting match or give yourself an anxiety attack.

I've found that it also pays to know my own limits when I'm in an uncomfortable situation that my faith simply hasn't had the need, or the opportunity, or even the ability to process. When a family stood over the dead body of their loved one in a hospital bed and said they were going to "ask Christ to raise him up, just like he did Lazarus," I had to leave the room. It was nineteen exhausting hours into a twenty-four-hour on-call shift, and I was not prepared to hear that. It was 3 a.m., the night had been busy, and I wasn't thinking straight. Truthfully, I was terrified they might succeed. What if these people prayed and that dead man sat up? What the hell would my circle-of-life pagan beliefs do with *that*? What would it mean for my faith? I offered my condolences and a prayer for God's presence with the family in their grief, but when they said they wanted to try to raise up the dead man, I had to book it.

I didn't hear about any resurrections at the hospital that night, and later I processed my feelings with my supervisor, but in the moment, the best thing I could do was leave. I didn't know how to be with a family whose greatest prayer was to literally bring their loved one back from the dead. I firmly believed that staying would not have served them, and leaving helped me keep my wits for the rest of my shift.

Now I know I should have stayed, to be with that family when God didn't answer their prayer the way they wanted him to. My job was to support their faith, but instead I let my own freakout decide for me: I thought of myself instead of the family. If I had it to do over, I would stand by them while they prayed and then wait to see if he would rise. I would hold them as they cried when he didn't.

Unitarian Universalists have long worked alongside Christians to further the social justice causes we all believe in. In 2013, Unitarian Universalists in North Carolina joined Christian justice advocates in protests at the state legislature. They rallied weekly against the Republican-dominated legislature's cuts to state social programs and public education, changes in voting and abortion rights, and the repeal of the landmark Racial Justice Act. And in February 2014, Unitarian Universalists from across the country joined twenty-two other faith-based agencies and congregations—plus dozens of other organizations—in the NAACP's annual Historic Thousands on Jones Street march in Raleigh. It was billed as the Moral March on Raleigh and as the largest march in the South since Selma. We marched for immigrants' and voters' rights, women's right to control our own bodies, the right of gay and lesbian couples to marry, and the right to a fair wage. The crowd was energized, chanting, singing, shouting, and waving signs.

My beloved and I were near the back of the march in a small sea of Unitarian Universalist friends and strangers, wearing our bright yellow Standing on the Side of Love gear and singing "Siyahamba (We Are Marching)." Our singing petered out, though, when I saw a man standing on the sidewalk and wearing a burlap sack over his clothes. He was shouting and holding a sign saying, "Abortion, adultery, homosexuality, sin. Repent. America's judgment is here."

The instant I read the sign, rage exploded in my chest. But just before I started shouting obscenities at him, I heard in my head what some of our organizers had advised before the march took off: If we are confronted with people spewing hate, respond with love. So, a millisecond before I would have screamed hate at this hate-filled man, I started singing at the top of my lungs: "We are standing on the side of love, we are standing on the side of love!"

Anger is such an amazingly visceral feeling—a feeling that can bubble up slowly, like a pot of water coming to a boil, or explode in an instant, like fireworks. If I hadn't heard the reminder to love just minutes before I saw that hate-filled man, I would have responded with self-righteous fury. I still nearly did. I sang loving words, but I sang them angrily. That day, it was the best I could do. It was good enough to sing words of love in an angry tone. It was good enough because it was better than saying any of the vitriol-laden things I thought about saying.

Life would be far easier if Unitarian Universalism were a faith that encouraged us to throw up our hands in resignation when faced with challenging people like the woman who disliked my bumper sticker, or people who use the Bible to justify intolerance, hate, and fear-mongering. Instead, our Sources remind us that the "Jewish and Christian teachings . . . call us to respond to God's love by loving our neighbors as ourselves." Those teachings are at the heart of historical Unitarianism and Universalism, and all too often we forget that they're included in our list of sources of wisdom and inspiration.

The two strands of our faith were deeply Christian, though radically so. The Unitarian firebrand William Ellery Channing spoke of the spiritual freedom Jesus came to give—freedom to believe as your heart and mind tell you to, rather than as the Church says you must; freedom to guard your intellect and spirit from forces aiming to conform it to their ideas; freedom to retain your own beliefs. And Hosea Ballou's doctrine of universalism stemmed from his belief that finite human beings were incapable of doing anything to offend the infinite God. That meant that the idea that Jesus died to atone for humanity's sins was a fallacy; for Ballou, God was loving and desired the happiness of his children for eternity.

Unitarian Universalists are amazingly welcoming to atheists, humanists, Buddhists, and pagans, yet when we face a Christian in the workplace, many of us draw back. We turn away. All too often, we do not even try to love our Christian neighbors as ourselves.

It's easy to understand why. Too many Unitarian Universalists have been hurt by warped versions of Christianity. Too many of us who are gay, lesbian, or transgender have been told we are not welcome in God's kingdom. Too many of our atheists, humanists, and pagans have been told we'll burn in hell.

The problem with this understandable reaction to painful experiences is that we live in a Christian country: a country founded on the principle of religious freedom, yes, but one in which the master narrative is still very much biblical. Each of us experiences this. We all know we have to navigate our liberal lives within a Christian context, often within a very conservative Christian context. Yet many Unitarian Universalists seem to think we can ignore that context as well as whatever unfortunate history we as individuals might have with Christian churches or their people.

The reality is that we have to find a way to be at peace with Christianity, or at least with the Christians we interact with every day—including the Christians in our families. I do not want Unitarian Universalism to be an exclusively Christian faith. I do not deny the pain caused when people twist the teachings of the Hebrew Bible and of Jesus to serve their own cruel purposes. I certainly do not defend it.

But. And.

We are called by our faith—in humanity, in the universe, in life itself—to try to see past the stated beliefs of people whose words incite outrage in our hearts. We must look to see how they use those beliefs in life: Are they able to put them aside and be with those they work with as equals, or do those beliefs hamper their ability to treat others with respect?

We must look to see what the beliefs do for them. Is the punishing, intolerant God a form of self-protection, reassurance that *someone* is looking out for them, even if that someone is a far-away God?

Many Unitarian Universalists lump all Christians into a single category, as though there aren't dozens of strains of Baptists alone. (I even have a dear friend who is—I swear—an ordained, liberal, lesbian Baptist!) We think their beliefs give them all the answers and make life easier to swallow, but I have found the opposite to be true. I mean, you try believing in a God who damns people to hell and then not living in fear that your beloved agnostic brother will go there when he dies. The conservative Christians I've worked with struggle with the meaning of life, illness, and death as much as any Unitarian Universalist I've met. Their theology is different, but their human experience is very much the same.

Coming to terms with our Christian heritage is crucial to our spiritual health. Serving as a chaplain in an overwhelmingly Christian setting has taught me how hard it is to respect others' beliefs when they're so different from my own, especially when those beliefs are fundamentally disrespectful of mine. I've encountered many people who say, flat-out, that their faith is the only way to live, the only way to salvation—the assumption being, of course, that we are all in need of salvation.

Yet when we move past rigid dogma and into personal conversation, I've been able to connect with them, often in deeply meaningful ways. Sharing our stories is how we open the hearts of others and ourselves. It's difficult to be pliable rather than rigid, but the trees that survive the storm are not the ones whose rigidity causes them to snap but those that bend with the winds.

It's not that I want to face my own prejudices. None of us does. Doing so means acknowledging my own ability to be bigoted, cruel, and closed-minded. Yet this is the paradox of my calling: I am called to chaplaincy work that forces me to confront my own intolerance for the intolerant. The call of Unitarian Universalism is for me to be more tolerant than those who refuse to tolerate me.

In his poem "Outwitted," Edwin Markham writes,

He drew a circle that shut me out—
Heretic, rebel, a thing to flout.
But Love and I had the wit to win:
We drew a circle that took him in!

Historically, Unitarian Universalists have been shut out of the circle, deemed heretics and heathens. We have accepted the mantle of outsider and relished it. Now we must learn to draw our circles larger, to draw others in, even those who talk about God at secular workplaces, even those who challenge our thoughts and, by doing so, invite us into deeper contemplation of what we know to be true.

What if we really are able to draw our circles so that our love can take all others in? Not into our congregations—that wouldn't make them any happier than it would us—but instead into conversation.

It is when we have the courage to risk genuine conversation that we begin to mend our individual hearts and the heart of Unitarian Universalism itself. We will know a fuller understanding of our shared humanity, in all our flawed perfection. Then and only then will we truly know the worth of ourselves and every person, even—maybe especially—those who disagree with us.

Empowering the Bereaved

REBEKAH INGRAM

Death is perhaps the most elusive yet definitive of human expe-riences, which we will all encounter one day. How and when will I die? What will it feel like? What will happen after I die? Most of us ask these questions at some point in our lives. None of us can answer them with certainty, although many of us have meaningful ideas, beliefs, and intuitions that help us craft answers to some, if not all, of them.

Those who care for the dying must frequently provide them with emotional, spiritual, and physical support. This can involve intensive medical and nursing interventions, or it can be a peaceful, loving presence at the bedside, a song, a prayer, or comforting words.

End-of-life care providers who regularly witness death often notice patterns in the dying process. These observations both challenge and contribute to our beliefs, pushing us to continu-ally search for meaning and understanding. Why did it hap-pen this way? Why is one death so different from or similar to another? Questions like these help caregivers cope with death and the ensuing grief. They are an attempt to call forth order and predictability where there is mystery. As human beings, we strive to understand the unexplainable, including death. We want to know why death and other unexplainable events hap-pen the way they do, so we can avoid them, or repeat them, or at least make some sense of them.

Having worked as a chaplain in both hospital and hospice settings, I have been privileged to attend deaths in a wide range of locations and circumstances. Because of this, my beliefs about death are largely rooted in my personal experiences and observations. Inspired by the individuals, families, and caregivers I work with, I am particularly interested in how people understand death from a religious, spiritual, or existential perspective and how these understandings come into being.

It amazes me how every person involved with a death can have a different perception and understanding of what occurred. A beautiful example of this was a death I attended when I was working with hospice. I had just visited with an elderly man and his spouse. The man was not verbal, but communicated with tremendous smiles. Shortly after his spouse left to return home, while I was at the nursing station, the man's nurse alerted me to the fact that his breathing had suddenly and drastically changed. He appeared to be dying, and very quickly. As word spread through the long-term care facility where this gentleman resided, caregivers gathered at his bedside. A message was left for his spouse, who had not yet returned home to answer the phone. In the next few minutes, his breathing slowed even more, until he took his last breath. We all waited in silence. One minute later, there was one final gasp and he was dead. I whispered an Episcopal prayer in his ear, someone else made the sign of the cross, another opened the window so his soul could depart, another closed his eyelids and said goodbye. This is a beautiful and embodied example of the religious and spiritual differences that were part of this man's death. I suspect that if we each (including the man who was dying) explained what was happening, there would be five different accounts of the same death.

I am intrigued by beliefs about death and how they shape end-of-life care and grief support in America. How do the deaths we witness shape our beliefs about death? What motivates us as caregivers to share our beliefs with others, particularly the bereaved with whom we work?

In my experiences with hospice care, my participation on a pain and palliative care team at a large teaching hospital in

Boston, and my subsequent collaborations with palliative care providers, I have learned how important it is for those who care for the dying to set aside time to reflect on the deaths they witness. They need an opportunity to process their observations, feelings, and questions. I have seen gatherings of hospice and palliative health care providers take place formally and informally, which, I believe, speaks to the importance of collectively practicing self-care. It is common to set aside time during interdisciplinary team meetings, or rounds, for remembering, sharing, and reflecting on the deaths that have been witnessed. Often, when care providers find themselves in the same space (and with some time and privacy), they will informally debrief, sharing their experiences. Whenever I have the opportunity to participate in these kinds of reflective gatherings, whether planned or impromptu, I am always humbled by the emotions and experiences that are shared, and how this is done with honesty and courage. These gatherings are places of healing: places where pain is softened and meaning is made. And on those occasions when there is little softening and not much meaning to be found, we can see that we are not alone in this intimate, deeply moving, inspiring, and even doubt-inducing work.

Certain beliefs about death and dying are often repeated by health care providers in both formal and informal conversations. It's as if caregivers, especially those who care for people at the ends of their lives, have become a faith community where such beliefs are shared. One example I often hear is the observation that people in the process of dying will die when they're ready. (This excludes sudden, unexpected deaths.) I've heard many accounts of children gathering at the bedside of a dying parent, with one child late to arrive because of the travel required. Shortly after that child arrives, the parent dies. It's as if the parent had been waiting for all their children to be present before transitioning from life to death.

Observations such as these are commonly discussed among care providers. They offer them to each other and to the dying and the grieving as a form of comfort and support. Shared beliefs about death create a framework and language for caregivers who attempt to understand that which is ultimately unknow-

able. These beliefs can normalize the dying process, which is
especially helpful when professional caregivers are teaching and
supporting the family and friends of the dying. The conclusions
we reach about death and dying give us a common language
and ontological grounding for how we understand the mysterious and often wondrous patterns observed in death and dying.
They might help us better understand why and how someone
dies. When someone waits until all their children are present
before dying, the caregivers might conclude that the person had
a peaceful death, maintaining autonomy up to the last breath,
choosing not to die until the children were there.

Maggie Callanan and Patricia Kelley are nurses who wrote
a book titled *Final Gifts: Understanding the Special Awareness,
Needs, and Communications of the Dying*, which examines end-of-
life patterns observed by caregivers who accompany the dying.
Highlighting a few of the observations from this book can demonstrate the framework of meaning that guides, informs, and
sustains many caregivers who tend to the dying and bereaved.
These are the beliefs that I hear most frequently when working
in hospice and palliative care. They are discussed among professional caregivers and they are also shared with the dying, their
families, and their friends as a way of providing information
about the dying process.

The first belief is about timing. It is often said that people
choose the timing of their death. This means that death might
happen on a day that is significant or on one that is purposefully
insignificant. Someone might die on their birthday, or wait until
the day after a holiday or anniversary so that a time of joy and
celebration is not forever paired with grief and loss.

Second, there are the surroundings. It is frequently observed
that people wait for their surroundings to be set up in a certain
way. This might mean the presence of familiar objects or music,
or for a religious practice to be carried out, particularly an end-
of-life ritual. Some choices involve both timing and surroundings, as when a dying person waits for certain family members
or friends to be either present in or absent from the room.

A third belief is that people die the way they lived. For example, a social and talkative person might remain verbal and main-

tain as many interactions as possible through the dying process, while an introvert might be quiet and become withdrawn early on, speaking and interacting only minimally with the living. The fourth belief is that people need permission to die, particularly from their family, friends, and caregivers. Time and time again, I hear that death does not occur until all family members have said goodbye and forgiveness has been received and given. The living might even encourage the person who is dying to let go of life and accept death. I have also heard how important it is to reassure a dying person that the family and friends left behind will be all right and that they will continue to look after one another. After these kinds of assurances have been spoken aloud, the dying person seems to accept death more peacefully and gracefully.

These beliefs about death are significant for those who accompany the dying, including family and caregivers. They can be comforting and reassuring; they help us ascribe meaning to what we witness. They make the dying process less frightening, especially to those who have not witnessed death before. This method of deriving meaning and wisdom from our personal experiences and observations is familiar to Unitarian Universalists, who consider personal experience, as well as reason and science, to be an important source of truth, faith, and theological grounding.

Drawing on their experience and observations, caregivers offer tremendous insight into the dying process. However, it is crucial that they assess when it is appropriate and helpful to offer their wisdom and when it is better to refrain from sharing. Caregivers must tend to their own grief, but they are also called upon to provide education, reassurance, comfort, and support to the grieving and bereaved, who may find comfort and meaning in very different ways than they do. As a Unitarian Universalist health care chaplain, I believe that caregivers can offer support in ways that honor all the differences that can be part of death and dying. This is no small task. Striving toward this end is crucial if we are to honor each person, acknowledge the complexities of grief, and celebrate the possibilities for healing. Here is an example of that striving.

A Mother and Her Son

I'm sitting at a large conference table with other members of the interdisciplinary team as we review each person we are caring for. The nurses express concern about a man named Jack who will not leave his dying mother's side. Furthermore, they are surprised by the mother's dying process. While no one can predict exactly when someone will die, there are some signs that indicate death's imminence. In this case, death is coming much more slowly than the mother's physiological signs suggest. Still, Jack does not leave her side. He appears distressed, and the care providers are struggling to find a way to help him. "Can you stop by and check on him?" they ask me. "We keep encouraging him to take a break, go home, and sleep, but he only leaves her side to get something quick to eat. He's been there for days and he's not looking well."

Concerned about the son and his dying mother, I wonder why this death is unfolding the way it is. Why is Jack reluctant to leave his mother's side? Why is she dying so slowly? I am curious if there is a way for him to feel more at ease. What compels him to sit vigil like this? I remind myself that care providers who regularly encounter death have a familiarity with dying that is not often shared by others. I am hoping there is a way for Jack's presence at his mother's bedside to bring peace and healing rather than concern and distress. Before I enter the mother's room, I take a deep breath, clearing my mind in order to see the situation before me with as little judgment and as few assumptions as possible.

After Jack and I have talked for a little while, he turns to me with a look of horror on his face and says, "Her providers say that she will choose when she dies, and that she might prefer to die without me here. So she may wait until I leave the room. Or maybe she wants me to stay by her side." He pauses. It seems that he has more to say, and I wonder where he is going with this. A few moments later he explains, "No one can believe that she's still alive. Her breaths are so far apart; the nurses say her blood pressure is really low. They keep asking me if I know why she's still hanging on. I have no idea. I can't think of anything."

Another long pause and then he asks me, "What am I supposed to do? If I leave, she might die, and if I stay, I'm prolonging her death and am the cause of her suffering."

I feel as if the breath has been knocked out of me as I realize the magnitude and source of Jack's distress. The caregivers told Jack that his mother would choose the time of her death in a sincere attempt to offer comfort and helpful information; however, this information is actually the source of Jack's distress. The difficulty is not his mother's dying, but rather the explanation of her dying process that he's been offered. Unfortunately, their wisdom renders Jack at once powerful and powerless. If he leaves, he could be the cause of her death. If he stays, he is the cause of her suffering. From Jack's perspective, his mother's life and impending death are held hostage by his actions and there is no way for him to step outside this terrible equation.

This case raises the question of when we should share our wisdom and when we should not. Providers of pastoral care must carefully consider this question in their ministries, and discerning its answer is challenging, because it requires intuition, humility, and accurate perceptions of self and others. It is not easy. We make mistakes. We don't always assess people and situations correctly. However, this should not prevent us from trying.

There are ways to cultivate and develop our pastoral skills so that they accurately respond to each person and situation, particularly at the end of a person's life. Pastoral care providers must pay attention to their own assumptions and ask questions of both themselves and those with whom they work and whom they serve. A pastoral care provider who approaches each person and situation with respectful curiosity, humility, self-awareness, and openness is working in the spirit of Unitarian Universalism. This pastoral model seeks to affirm and promote the worth and dignity of all, honoring the many truths, questions, and doubts each of us encounters. When we believe that each person's experiences are unique and that each person deserves the freedom to make sense and meaning in ways that are true and meaningful for them, then we are thoughtful and intentional about sharing our own beliefs. The greatest risk we take when we share our beliefs in a pastoral setting is that we might do so in ways that limit diversity, silence difference, and create distress. Pastoral care that does this contradicts our Unitarian Universalist faith. It is oppressive and limiting, for it diverts people from their own spiritual and emotional journeys and all the uniqueness, pain, and beauty these journeys can contain.

In order to increase our skills and abilities as care providers who embrace differences, affirm the breadth of human experience, and recognize the worth and dignity of each person, I offer two pastoral guideposts, which are rooted in my Unitarian Universalist faith and inform my ministry as a chaplain.

First, we must pay close attention to our assumptions. What do we presume to be true about others' beliefs, values, and priorities? This is an important question to regularly ask of ourselves and everyone we encounter in a pastoral situation. It is natural to make assumptions and draw conclusions from the information we observe, intuit, and are told; however, the more we question and learn about the assumptions we inevitably make in any interaction and conversation, the more accurate our assessments and responses will be.

Second, we must ask questions. Whenever any needs or beliefs are expressed in a pastoral encounter (whether verbally or nonverbally), it is important for the care provider to understand their origins and meanings. In so doing, the provider is both practicing self-awareness and demonstrating a respectful curiosity that welcomes difference, diversity, and the unique experiences of every person.

Humbly asking questions and showing a respectful curiosity conveys a sense of welcome. When health care providers ask questions about more than just physical symptoms, they are letting the patient know that all of them is important, not just their body. The same is true at the bedside of someone who is dying. While certain patterns and emotions are common parts of the grieving process, it is important to remember that each person's grief and experiences of death are unique, including our own. When we find ourselves either hearing or sharing wisdom, we must ask ourselves, whose wisdom is this? Where does it come from, with whom shall I share it, and why? These are some of the most important questions I ask of myself and of those I encounter in a pastoral setting. Whose wisdom is this? Is it biblical, theological, religious, cultural, familial, or personal? Is it helping or is it harming?

When Jack was sitting with his dying mother, for example, caregivers made a number of assumptions. First, it is unclear whether the mother's process of dying was distressing to Jack before the caregiver described it as "slow." If Jack had not thought of it that way before the caregivers called his attention to their own observations and worries, their assumption about the appropriate speed of his mother's dying process, then they were responsible for introducing a perception that became a source of concern and confusion for him. But their aim is to companion people who are in distress and mitigate that distress when possible, not to introduce it or increase it.

When we observe someone to be in distress and feel distressed ourselves, it's important to remember that the causes of our distress may not be the same. The caregivers were perplexed by the mother's "slow" dying process and by Jack's reluctance to leave her side. Their second assumption was that the two were related, which was not necessarily the case. Once distress of any kind is recognized, it is essential to identify its source. In end-of-life situations, it is easy to conclude that the sources of all distress are the impending death, the losses that have already occurred and very likely led up to the dying process, and the sometimes daunting task of caring for and being a companion to someone who is dying.

A wide range of intense emotions is to be expected at the end of life. This is also a time when conclusions can be quickly drawn; however, it is crucial that health care providers pay attention to the assumptions underlying them. The nuances of each person's distress in the context of death and dying are often unique and may not be readily apparent. Thus, in every pastoral situation, we must ask ourselves how well we understand the sources of distress. For example, if Jack is distressed, have we asked him why, so that he can explain his emotions in his own words, with his own history, beliefs, experiences, and understanding welcomed into the conversation? The caregivers are distressed by what they see as the slow process of Jack's mother's dying. Jack, on the other hand, is distressed about being either the cause of his mother's death or the cause of her suffering. These are two profoundly different distresses that have arisen from one situation. First we must accurately perceive and assess the needs in a pastoral situation, and then we must learn more about them.

Next, Jack and the caregivers alike assume that there must be a reason why Jack's mother is dying at the speed she is. But there may be no reason, or the reason may be impossible to know. While those who work with the dying can become incredibly adept at predicting the end of someone's life, it behooves us to remember that no one can do so with complete certainty. The comfort that Unitarian Universalists have with questions and doubts is especially helpful as we embrace the fact that her "slow" dying process may remain unexplainable. There may not be a medical or biological explanation. If there is an emotional, social, or spiritual explanation, we cannot know it.

Lastly, the caregivers assume that Jack should be able to answer their questions: that Jack, as a son, should know his mother well enough to know why her death is unfolding the way it is and that he should feel comfortable sharing this with her caregivers. What is concerning about these assumptions is that they are grounded in an expectation that Jack's relationships with his mother and her caregivers are supposed to involve a significant amount of trust and openness. If Jack cannot offer the explanations the caregivers ask for from him, he may naturally conclude that he doesn't have the kind of relationship with his mother that they expect him to, and perhaps even that he has failed his mother in some way or is not living up to his role as a son.

The caregivers' questions suggest that Jack is supposed to know why his mother is dying slowly. It is the caregivers, not Jack, who need to know why her death is slow. It's interesting to note that Jack's only question is, What do I do? He does not ask why. Naturally, the caregivers are focused on the slowness of Jack's mother's dying because it is the part of her death that they find unusual, that is difficult for them to understand and explain. They assume that there is a reason for this slowness, that it is knowable, and that it is knowable by Jack. However, none of this is so. Jack's questions are about what he can do to support and care for his mother at the end of her life. Unfortunately, the caregivers' wisdom has unintentionally and unexpectedly placed a tremendous amount of responsibility on Jack's shoulders. He is not comfortable remaining at his mother's bedside and he is not comfortable leaving. What, then, can he do?

The case of Jack and his mother is an important example of how sharing one's own wisdom, beliefs, and insight can prevent others from engaging in spiritual and emotional work that relates to their experiences. It can disempower rather than empower. It can blur the boundary between the caregivers' needs and the patient or family's needs.

Here is where Unitarian Universalism is especially helpful. We celebrate diversity and support each person on their spiritual journey, which is not ours to judge or critique. On this basis, would it be possible to simply perceive Jack's mother's death as unique to her, rather than as atypical in its slowness? It's a subtle but important semantic distinction. Is it unique, or is it atypical and slow? When we use words that suggest something is not normal, such as *atypical*, we open the way to worries that might not otherwise have arisen. If something is not normal, then something is wrong. There are certainly times when it is helpful to share thoughts and questions with those who are grieving and bereaved, but when they become a distraction, or when they express the caregiver's needs rather than the bereaved person's, then we run into trouble. The more able we are as caregivers to welcome differences, therefore, the less likely we are to put our judgment on someone else. The more adept we are at recognizing our own feelings and what we find unsettling about a given situation, the less likely we are to put our needs upon someone else, especially all those who are sitting vigil at the bedsides of the dying.

If Unitarian Universalists are committed to promoting and affirming the inherent worth and dignity of each person, then we must also recognize that this Principle emphasizes the uniqueness of each person. Our Unitarian Universalist faith does not specify which elements or aspects of each person merit worth and dignity. Our First Principle does not provide a shared, generalized definition of worth and dignity. It doesn't tell us how to promote and affirm them. And so each person must explore and apply this Principle using their own intellect, reason, knowledge, experiences, and intuition. This implies that all human beings are unique in how they might understand and apply this Principle. Unitarian Universalism emphasizes individuality within community and in relationship.

If each person is unique, particularly in how they choose to live in this world and be in relationship and community with others, then each dying process and each death is unique. Caregivers who recognize this will be especially careful when they describe death. They would be wise to refrain from sharing subjective perceptions that close the door to other interpretations. Jack's distress is an example of what can happen when caregivers share their beliefs about and understandings of death in ways that are limiting. Jack is not able to disagree with the caregivers' perception of his mother's death as "slow." He is not able to disagree with them when they inform him that his mother will choose when she dies and that her choice is very likely linked to his presence at her bedside.

I have found it helpful to invite family and friends to share their observations of the dying process in ways that make sense to them, their family, and their communities, using their own culture, language, narratives, religious or spiritual beliefs, and knowledge of the person who is dying. Reminding family members that each person's dying is unique and asking them how they are experiencing it is one way to empower and welcome them, and it enables care providers to offer compassionate care that is appropriate and responds to the unique needs of each person rather than being formulaic, judgmental, presumptuous, or addressed to the care provider's own needs.

Paying attention to their own assumptions and asking questions helps chaplains and other caregivers assess a pastoral situation. Most importantly, doing so encourages chaplains to assess both what is within and what is without. It is crucial that in pastoral encounters we not let our needs interfere with the needs of those we are caring for. Practices that promote self-awareness during a pastoral encounter enable us to recognize what is ours and place it appropriately aside. When we struggle to separate our needs from the needs of others during a pastoral encounter, we learn something incredibly important: We need to step back and take care of ourselves before we can care for another. This could mean taking a break or even referring the case to another pastoral care provider. Our assessments and the care we provide are inextricably tied to our self-assessment and self-care practices. Because of this, asking questions of ourselves and of others and paying attention to assumptions are key components of pastoral care that is patient-centered, need-based, and empowering.

Like their birth, each person's death is unique. Human beings are unique in body and mind, in spirit and soul. Unitarian Universalism honors the uniqueness of all beings. In this way, our faith calls us out of expectation and assumption. It calls us to look for all the ways a person or situation is unique and to embrace this sacred uniqueness rather than fearing and judging it. We are quick to seek understanding, slow to judge. At least, that is my hope for Unitarian Universalists, particularly those who care for the dying, the grieving, and the bereaved.

Serving a Collective Mission

CYNTHIA L. G. KANE

My call to serve as a US Navy chaplain presented itself to me as a spiritual call like any other. A significant amount of sober thought and deliberation went into the decision. After all, from the start of ministerial training, I had intended to enter campus chaplaincy. I loved university life and thrived within it, I understood its rhythms and idiosyncrasies, and I greatly appreciated its occasional anarchies. Military ministry was neither the goal I envisioned when I entered divinity school, nor the goal that my loved ones envisioned for me. So it took a good deal of discussion and reflection to translate my first clear intimation of a future in military service into the act of inking my signature on the Department of Defense's Form DD1—the commission form that every officer of every branch of the US military has signed.

Nevertheless, it was not a rational discussion or calculation that brought me to service as a naval chaplain. Nor was it September 11, 2001. My military service began in 1996, in the midst of a rare period of international hopefulness. The collapse of the Soviet Union (and with it the Cold War) was several years behind us; the European Union's experiment with internal open borders was taking shape; and the Truth and Reconciliation process in post-apartheid South Africa had begun to offer the world a new model for moving beyond even the most psychologically searing forms of conflict.

That's not to say all was well around the globe. The genocide in Rwanda, with its stupefying pace of slaughter—more than eight hundred thousand people killed in a hundred days—was fresh in memory. So was the multiyear campaign of ethnic cleansing in the former Yugoslavia, and it was far from clear that the 1995 Dayton Accords would be able to permanently quell the conflict. Also still fresh in memory was the 1993 World Trade Center bombing, though in most Americans' minds, including my own, it was hardly a harbinger of struggles to come.

Yet none of these events affected my decision to put aside, for an unknown stretch of years, my vision of a life in campus ministry. At least, they did not do so in any way I can access or track. Readers may well differ on the question of whether true spiritual callings are possible, whether the Divine can actually enter our lives to communicate—unmistakably and unignorably—that we need to look at what's behind door number two, even if we had our hearts set on door one or three. Many will assume that callings are in fact the product of the unconscious mind as it seeks to make sense of events, whether personal or geopolitical, and presents its conclusions in an irrefutable form.

To those who doubt the possibility of a calling, I can only say that I felt called to do this work. I believe I was called to do it. And to those who believe in its possibility but have trouble imagining a call to military ministry, I can only say that mine was a calling like any other. My vision of campus ministry faded, and at age twenty-eight I began to contemplate instead the joys of Officer Candidate School (OCS).

So I found myself entering the Navy in 1996, as the first Unitarian Universalist to serve in active duty since the Korean War and one of the few female chaplains of any faith tradition in any of the US armed forces. I would be working primarily with the same age group I had been eager to minister to in campus settings, but within a wholly different framework. Indeed, my generally left-of-center politics and peacenik bona fides, among other things, made many of the young people I encountered view me with either curiosity or suspicion.

(My naval career was put on hold before it ever officially started. The day after graduating divinity school, I was diagnosed with an exceptionally rare form of cancer. I spent the next two years recovering, then another three getting back into the Navy. I finally was commissioned on August 21, 2001.)

I experienced September 11, 2001, from the vantage point of a naval lieutenant, junior grade (O-2). Many of the young men and women I ministered to found themselves mobilizing for a war they never could have foreseen. Shortly thereafter came a wave of enlistees who had been motivated to serve in the wake of 9/11, or who had been on the enlistment track before the tragic events of that day but sought to invest their service with new meaning in its wake.

By 2004, I found myself posted to a chaplaincy at Guantanamo Bay, in the immediate aftermath of the troubling revelations of abuse at Abu Ghraib. For months, I walked the cellblocks where male detainees, primarily Muslim, were housed. Ostensibly I was there to provide a calming pastoral presence, yet just by being an American woman in military uniform wearing the sign of the cross I was a provocation. A little more than a decade later, as a purveyor of the open and affirming stance of Unitarian Universalism, I find myself "stationed" in a very different sort of contested terrain, asked to participate in policy making and culture change as the armed forces scrambled to respond to the collapse of Don't Ask, Don't Tell and the Defense of Marriage Act. Yet, nearly two decades after completing OCS, I also serve alongside a vibrant and growing cadre of fellow Unitarian Universalist clergy.

As I reflect on doing ministry in a nonreligious institution, I find myself returning to a single, central theme of my time in the vast and complex institution that is the US Navy: My service has been nothing so much as an ongoing act of translation. It has been a process of translating Unitarian Universalism to the Navy, from which Unitarian Universalism had been largely absent for decades after the Korean War; translating between and among various religious positions and worldviews; and translating the meaning of a life in military service to the Unitarian Universalist community, which has not always been eager to understand us.

Finding a Common Grammar

Without pushing the metaphor of translation too far, before I could grow into a role focused largely on bridging and interpreting a wide range of faith traditions and worldviews within a complex institutional setting, I had to master some important lessons in the common grammar that makes translation possible in the US military context. These lessons are best explained in story form.

My first assignment in the Navy was in Washington, D.C., where my supervisory chaplain was hard-core, old-school, and Southern Baptist. He had never heard of Unitarian Universalism, let alone met a Unitarian Universalist! Our first meetings might easily have been filmed as a sitcom. On one side of the table, the new officer, a female chaplain, representing a faith that to her superior officer likely seemed amorphous and doctrineless. On the other, a seasoned military chaplain, veteran of every conflict since Vietnam, who paired the discipline of a rigid military hierarchy with the discipline of his own staunchly conservative belief system. We struggled to find common ground when discussing the needs of our largely young-adult flock, the contours of ministry, and the interplay of military and spiritual needs and demands. Finding common theological ground was completely impossible.

Yet that seasoned chaplain fervently believed in one thing, neither military nor spiritual in nature, which formed the basis of our work together. This was the unequivocal call of the First Amendment. For him, the First Amendment mandated that however we agreed or disagreed over matters of ministry and theology, his role was to help me, the military's lone Unitarian Universalist clergy member, build a framework for my ministry. This would allow service members who found Unitarian Universalist tenets compatible with their spiritual needs to find support, whether from me directly or from a larger Unitarian Universalist presence we both hoped would eventually emerge.

Our relationship grew with time, and we gained respect for each other's ministry and commitments to our service members. Eventually, he became one of Unitarian Universalism's greatest allies in the Navy. On transferring to Great Lakes Naval Training Center, where all Navy recruits report for basic training, he noticed right away that there was no Unitarian Universalist representation within the command religious program. Without any fanfare, he proceeded to recruit two Meadville Lombard seminarians to begin a weekly Unitarian Universalist service. For the first several weeks, chairs at these services were mostly empty; but as word spread, attendance swelled to regular crowds of eighty or more. For the past decade, thousands of new sailors have thus gained access to support and fellowship in a Unitarian Universalist context during the arduous process of basic training.

In describing his First Amendment convictions as the platform for our shared work, I by no means wish to paper over the serious critiques of and legal challenges that have been brought against the US armed forces. Across all service branches there have been reports of the marginalization of nondominant faiths. For instance, evangelical Christianity has been said to enjoy an entrenched, favored status at the Air Force Academy, and the Navy has been accused (in *Adair v. England* [2002]) of allocating a disproportionately low number of chaplaincy positions to nonliturgical Christian clergy, relative to the number of Navy service members who identify as nonliturgical Christians.

Yet in the military—as in all institutions—there is a noticeable disjuncture between the practices of administrative elites and daily practices "on the ground." In my own nearly two decades in the Navy, I have found other chaplains, including superior officers in chaplaincy commands, to be forthrightly committed to helping lay roots for Unitarian Universalist ministry. They are not always motivated, as my first supervisory chaplain was, by high regard for the First Amendment. Some may be motivated by official Department of Defense policy, which emphasizes the importance of religious diversity and religious accommodation. Others may be motivated by formal or informal tenets of collegiality, or by their own intuition that supporting chaplains of other faiths—particularly ones who can minister to those whose dog tags are stamped NRP, "no religious preference"—will help to build a stronger, more resilient Navy.

The bottom line is that the platform for our work together has not always been interfaith dialogue or even shared respect for or knowledge of each other's faith traditions. Instead, our shared nonreligious frameworks of law, policy, professionalism, and practical concern for the needs of service people drive our day-to-day cooperation. My first supervisory chaplain articulated a neutral basis for our work together with particular clarity. In other assignments, it has taken more time to tease out. But by taking time to identify such shared, secular, motivational norms, it becomes possible to emphasize them and enlarge them, and thereby open more room for outsider forms of ministry, such as mine was at the beginning. Moreover, it become possible to strengthen the case for pluralism and interfaith cooperation, on the basis of the institution's own norms and practices.

Translating under Stress: The Guantanamo Bay Experience

It might seem at the outset that the crucial form of "translation" that occurred in the Guantanamo context would have been between Christians and Muslims, yet there was no room for anything so exalted. As mentioned above, I was assigned to Guantanamo Bay in the wake of the Abu Ghraib revelations. As part of an overall strategy to minimize the potential for more such abuses, the US military sought to enhance the visible presence of clergy at Guantanamo. It was hoped the visible presence of clergy would help to promote reflection and caution, even among service members who do not regularly seek ministerial guidance—that they would be reminded of their own ethical and moral codes before sliding into the type of behaviors that had shocked the world. To a certain extent, we were there to operate as moral speed bumps, if not stop signs.

The pressures on personnel at Guantanamo were enormous. Even absent the intense, global scrutiny directed at us in the wake of Abu Ghraib, it would have been difficult to serve detainees in even the smallest ways. The base was overcrowded but arguably understaffed. Air and sea transport to and from the facility was spotty, and media personnel were demanding more and more of the available transport resources, putting additional pressure on already-burdened supply lines. Meanwhile, a number of the detainees—primarily radicalized Muslims detained in connection with the wars in Afghanistan and Iraq—were engaged in an ongoing, low-level struggle against military personnel, using any tools at their disposal.

For instance, one of my tasks was to make daily walking rounds of the cellblocks where detainees were housed. Most days, I received the "special treatment"—having feces, urine, spit, and semen hurled at me. It was a visceral form of protest against my presence as a female, a US Navy officer, and a chaplain who bore the sign of the cross.

Meanwhile, I was being watched and guarded primarily by eighteen- to twenty-year-old American males, many of whom had been raised in evangelical or Catholic households with strict codes of masculinity. Managing my own response to the actions of the detainees was secondary to managing the anger and protective instinct these actions provoked among young male service members.

Here I began to understand the unique capacity of the Unitarian Universalist belief system to help manage conflict and negotiate difference. Unlike many faiths, Unitarian Universalism offers not only a guide to our own behavior toward ourselves and others, but also a framework for understanding and contextualizing the behaviors of others. Its lineages are far closer than those of most religions to such secular disciplines as human rights law and humanistic psychology. Hence Unitarian Universalist prayer, meditation, and practice can lead directly to the type of social insight needed to defuse conflict in social and institutional settings.

Early on, as I realized the challenge of relating to detainees at Guantanamo, I meditated specifically on the Principles of the dignity of each human life and the right of conscience. In fairly short order, I found myself better able to contextualize and cope with the extreme behaviors of detainees, to understand how actions so clearly meant to humiliate me could be rational and even driven by conscience. In fact, members of the US military are also instructed to torment their captors if taken as prisoners of war. That tormenting was analogous to the harassment directed at me. The "special treatment" was just one form of it. Another occurred when a habeas corpus lawyer sent me a Bible, a thesaurus, and two volumes of Shakespeare, with the request that I pass them on to a specific detainee. Luckily, it was never my decision whether or not to pass materials on to detainees— I merely forwarded the package to the command's legal team. However, this too was likely a tactic of humiliation: if I failed to deliver the books, I and the United States could have been critiqued in the press for failing to deliver humanitarian aid to detainees (as in fact happened); but if I had passed the materials on, we could have been critiqued for insensitive religious and cultural proselytization.

Making direct connections with the detainees was, a priori, out of the question, and that was never part of my charge as a chaplain at Guantanamo. However, defusing tensions was. By meditating on central Unitarian Universalist tenets, I was able to gain conceptual purchase on the actions of detainees, which in turn helped me to set an example for, and guide and respond to, the younger, more reactive military personnel around me.

It may seem odd, but I did not at the outset try to engage US personnel by asking them to consider our common humanity with the detainees. I merely asked them to consider the ways that we ourselves had been trained to respond when taken captive. From that moment of translation and equivalency, others followed. Even the most patriotic and hawkish of the young people to whom I minister understand that war causes us to behave in ways that flout our own senses of humanity. They understand this better than any civilian.

The Ministering to the NRPs at Guantanamo Bay

If asking service members to consider their own likely actions as prisoners of war represents translation at a primarily conceptual level, there were other, more pragmatic forms of bridging that were crucial to ministry at Guantanamo. I do not have data on the religious affiliations of the military personnel posted there, but they likely resemble the general military population, which is fairly diverse. Without a doubt, Christians represent the lion's share of the population; however, a dizzying variety of Christian groups are represented in the forces, along with scores of other faiths, including Judaism (likely around 1% of the total armed forces population), Islam (likely around 0.6%), and paganism (likely between 0.4% and 1%).

However, significant numbers within each service branch report no religious preference. These NRPs represent nearly 30 percent of enlisted personnel under age forty, according to a 2010 study by the Military Leadership Diversity Commission. This proportion is in keeping with national trends, which suggest that young people are increasingly likely to identify as NRPs or "nones." Yet the NRP population is by no means devoid of spiritual leanings or commitments. Indeed, less than 4 percent of all service members self-report as atheist or agnostic (coded as "humanist"), according to the study.

This population represents a particular challenge as large institutions seek to offer ministerial support to their members or clients, because they may be resistant to seeking guidance from traditional Catholic or Protestant clergy. The number of service members who affiliate and identify as Unitarian Universalist is miniscule. Yet the comparatively flexible Unitarian Universalist worldview, with its incorporation of diverse influences, including secular ones, may allow Unitarian Universalist ministers to reach populations of NRPs with particular efficacy.

We are, as a group, also uniquely poised to help the military understand the spiritual needs of NRPs—including, as odd as it may sound, the "spiritual" needs of atheists and agnostics, who may eschew formal ministry, particularly any that relies on a concept of divinity. Yet in the incomparably stressful and challenging context of war, even agnostic and atheist service people may want pastoral care and guidance in philosophical reflection; they may in fact rely on it, given the stigma that continues to exist around psychological counseling for active service members.

In the context of Guantanamo, therefore, I became particularly invested in ensuring that service members who did not routinely reach out for ministerial guidance felt invited to do so,

at whatever level of intensity worked for them. One of the most
visible outcomes of this drive was the "Chapulance"—an ambulance I retrofitted to provide a calm space where service members could hang out and chat about what was on their mind.
The Chapulance allowed me to perform outreach in all corners
of the base, including the places where the most routine opera-
tions took place, rather than expecting the flock to come to me.
Because if the faithful tend to flock, the less strongly affiliated
tend to spread out. Institutions must be reminded to meet them
where they are, and Unitarian Universalist ministers must be
part of that effort, no matter the institutional context.

Translating to the People Who Speak My Own Language

Intriguingly, in many respects it has been easier to translate the
work of Unitarian Universalism to the military than vice versa.
The support commanding officers have given me as a Unitarian
Universalist should not come as a surprise. Particularly given
the increasing numbers of NRPs, the armed services increasingly understand the importance of chaplains who can minister
in nontraditional ways and bridge diverse constituencies and
worldviews.

Conversely, I have often been unpleasantly surprised by
how difficult it can be to get fellow Unitarian Universalists to
accept my military work. Indeed, when I began to contemplate
military ministry, the idea provoked various shades of hostility,
ranging from disdain to outrage, among many of my colleagues
and divinity school classmates. Early in my career, I found it
impossible to convince nonmilitary Unitarian Universalists to
take seriously things I had learned, through my own experience, about some military processes. For instance, I considered
much of the Unitarian Universalist advocacy for detainees at
Guantanamo to be misguided, based on faulty evidence and
preconceptions. But when I offered to share my firsthand view
of the situation on the base with the Unitarian Universalist Service Committee (UUSC), I had difficulty gaining even a friendly
ear. One of my central missions in ministry is to interpret mili-

tary culture to civilian Unitarian Universalists, so that they can come to understand the aspects of it that are life-affirming and directed toward peace. And one way I channel this mission is through the humble and pan-contextual notion of service.

Just before I left for my first deployment, a sociologist friend explained to me Erving Goffman's concept of "total institutions." Goffman argued that some institutions—most especially prisons and military institutions—are intended to remake people. All the markers of personal identity are stripped away on entering: inductees give up their clothes, submit to a standardized haircut, eat the institution's food, submit to its schedule. There was, truly, something profound about the process of entering the military. I found myself bonding with the other chaplains in my basic training course in a way that outstripped anything I experienced in college or graduate school. We chaplains were forced to put aside differences in order to concentrate on fulfilling each task given to us and on functioning as smoothly as possible.

I know the criticisms of this remaking. It has been argued that service people lose the ability to think critically, that they forgo moral decision making. However, the people with whom I serve also have a quality that many of those in civilian life lack. Where civilians prize individuality above almost anything else, service people believe in the importance of acting as a unit. The beauty of such action rarely is recognized outside of military life. But how many of us have worked with groups to tackle important social issues, only to watch them falter and fail because of internal, often petty, conflicts?

One of the few places we can look for examples of subjugation of one's own needs to the collective goal is the deployed combat unit. The military is as filled with career concerns as any institution. But when a mission is at stake, that mission becomes paramount; loyalty and unity become the arbiters of life and death; and conflicts in personality and ideology are put aside in order to get the job done. It is an aspect of service that never ceases to inspire me, and there are many in the military who embrace it, not because they love war, but because they yearn for security and peace. It reminds me daily of what service means in any context, and it makes me wonder if there is room in progressive politics—where the individual's needs and goals have come to represent the highest ideal—to reengage with the idea of collective mission. This is a new type of Rosetta Stone I am working to craft.

I am not sure what a peacenik total institution would look like, but I suspect that many of us actually yearn to feel integrated into a more purposeful whole.

While simultaneously carrying out these various acts of institutional translation I have, of course, also been translating on a far more intimate, internal level, seeking to bridge and balance the two distinct callings I have encountered in my life: one to ministry within a tradition that places the utmost faith in peace and coexistence, and one to ministry within an institution of war. As I have suggested, these positions are not as inherently opposed as many might believe. However, the tension between them is ineradicable.

In this regard I face the same task that every military chaplain faces: to wear my dual insignia with conviction. To the right of my collar are the insignia of my military rank. To the left is the device of my chaplaincy, the cross.[1]

---

1   While Unitarian Universalism is not a Christian faith and does not usually use the cross as a symbol, it is a reliable visual indicator of my role. I was raised as a Christian and gravitated to Unitarian Universalism partly because of its Christian roots, and my theological framework is primarily rooted in Christianity, so I am comfortable with it. And in the military context, it is a wiser choice than the flaming chalice. Military culture relies on almost instant recognition of countless symbols and abbreviations; fellow servicemembers would likely interpret a flaming chalice to mean that I was a member of the Explosives Ordnance Division. My collar device, you might say, represents an initial act of translation.

Military Chaplaincy, A Natural Fit

XOLANI KACELA

About ten months after completing my application to serve as a chaplain in the Air National Guard, a component of the U.S. Air Force, I was told to report to duty on drill weekend, or Uniform Training Assembly. Within a couple hours, I was at a unit cookout, sitting among people I'd never met, getting to know them, and doing actual chaplain ministry. I didn't even have a uniform yet.

It is rare for aspiring military chaplains to have as smooth a transition as I did. But it seemed that the stars were perfectly aligned for me to be commissioned. Much of my process was facilitated by my predisposition to the military, my prior exposure to military people and procedures, and a future-oriented and positive mindset. I also tend to be fairly well-organized. Other traits suitable for military chaplains include assertiveness, physical fitness, and flexibility.

Some of my experience can be attributed to being born into a military family. My father was an Army man, who served for twenty-two years and did several combat tours. Our family moved a lot when I was young between various military posts in the South. Every other year, I went to a different school until I was in fifth grade, so I was exposed to many different cultures, lifestyles, dialects, races, and ethnicities. And as a teenager, I worked at Fort Benning in Georgia at the Army & Air Force Exchange Service (AAFES), a quasi-military, governmental agency that runs retail stores on military bases around the globe. This position put me in touch with soldiers and the military lifestyle at a time when I was impressionable. It further developed my positive bias toward the military. The environment at Fort Benning had something worldly about it. The young soldiers would come and go from the store with an air of manliness and free-spiritedness that I admired.

Later, as an adult, after graduating from college with a business degree, I again went to work for AAFES, this time as an internal auditor. My professional life at AAFES shaped my understanding of the military in profound ways. The experience provided a lens through which I could see the common humanity between the military and civilians.

Through my connections to the military, I've always lived in a multicultural environment. I haven't had to seek it out. Many Unitarian Universalists, on the other hand, have not had a multicultural upbringing—which includes interaction with military personnel. Most Unitarian Universalists are isolated from those who take up the profession of arms and, for the most part, do not understand the military.

Unitarian Universalists tend to see the military as a great behemoth that prevents the government from spending money on education, jobs, social programs, infrastructure, and other entitlements. We don't view the military as the government's arm of defense and national security that ensures our freedoms of liberty, justice, and religion. This bias handicaps our congregations, causing us to view military personnel and their families as the "other." It also presents a hurdle for veterans and families who might be open to joining our houses of worship. It can prevent us from appreciating military people and making sound use of their experience in our governance at the local level. Unitarian Universalists in congregations located near military installations are often exceptions to this overall trend. In any case, since I had a positive bias, I was open to working in the military from the start.

There were many intervening years between when I worked for AAFES and when I became a military chaplain. During that time, many of the values that I adopted have solidified and expanded. Most prominently, perhaps, is my awareness of our need, as a nation, for a standing military. My study of religious and theological history demonstrated over and over again the profound human tendency toward war. Regardless of the political philosophy of the leaders who are in power, the need for protection persists. That is the basic mandate of government: to protect its citizens. The primary means of carrying this out is through a trained, standing, and prepared military force.

The day that I was sworn in as an Air Force officer in 2002 was an emotional high. I felt like I was born again! I didn't take any family or friends with me to the event because no one seemed to make a big deal out of it. As in most work settings, the level of excitement around events like this depends largely on one's relationships in the organization. Since I had few relationships in the Air Force then, there was little made of the ceremony. Plus, in the military, they have events like this so often that on some level, you are just a number. In other words: Get in line, suck up it, and get it done. Still, the ceremony was transformative for me because I knew it represented a new beginning in a world with a rich tradition and heritage. The atmosphere in a military unit, with the fast tempo, decorum, and organizational structure, sends a message to its members that great things are possible and that you are a part of an organization with a purpose. As a service member, big things are expected of you. The commissioning process and swearing in brings all this to the fore of one's awareness.

Multicultural Competency

Being a military officer demands multicultural competency. The Air Force, like each of the services, has its own culture. You have to adapt quickly and find ways to assimilate or become a perpetual outsider. People who learn the culture and adapt to it will have a higher chance of success than those who resist assimilation and decide that they can change the culture. Of course, there are some who manage to change aspects of military culture, such as the leaders who implemented racial integration in military ranks and, more recently, those who made significant changes to the sexual assault policies. But, by and large, military organizations change individuals rather than the other way around.

The multicultural competencies needed for the military are similar to those necessary in Unitarian Universalism. Successful ministers learn how to develop relationships, cooperate with others in a mutually respectful way, and utilize the gifts and talents of all persons. Ministers who do not play by these rules tend to encounter much resistance.

Working with people of diverse backgrounds—racially, ethnically, culturally, socio-economically, etc.—is inevitable as a military officer. As a working/middle class person of color who grew up during desegregation, I've lived amid diverse populations all my life. I'm sort of a cultural chameleon; I know how to blend in, yet assert myself as needed. My Clinical Pastoral Education training as a hospital chaplain has helped me navigate the hierarchy and power dynamics of the military. Without it, I might have found myself struggling with the barriers of the armed forces culture, such as its strict command structure. The culture demands that people fall in line, accept commands, do as they are told by their superiors, or face the consequences. This can be challenging for many. But, once you figure out its purpose, you can respect the system, welcome it, and move on with your life. It is not the place to work out your unresolved power issues.

Another requirement of military life is learning the language. Military courtesy, acronyms, time, and the particular jargon used to describe formations, equipment, and everyday life are fairly complex. This language requirement is a multicultural competence in itself. Without skills in this area (which I am constantly learning), you can find yourself at a serious disadvantage in certain contexts, such as deployment and security briefings, technical schools, and everyday conversation.

Interfaith Ministry

When I was in the war zone during Operation Iraqi Freedom in 2010, I served as senior hospital chaplain in the Theater Hospital at Joint Base Balad, Iraq. As one of a twelve-member chapel team, I was assigned the traditional Protestant Sunday worship service held in the hospital. Each chaplain is responsible for developing and coordinating all the worship elements of the services to which they are assigned. This meant that I needed to offer a worship service with a traditional Christian message. The congregants of that service—hospital staff, patients, and civilians—came from a variety of Protestant backgrounds. Although I am a Unitarian Universalist, they expected me to preach sermons that focused on familiar topics such as Jesus and salvation, and to help them deal with struggles in that context. And so I conducted my services using language they were accustomed to. The worship was more for the worshippers than for the officiant. I have enough spiritual maturity so that however a service goes, my heart and soul are filled.

This is one thing that I adore about our Unitarian Universalist faith: We have the flexibility to use a full range of sources for religious services. This makes Unitarian Universalist ministers a lovely fit for military chaplaincy—provided that we embrace a full range of religious experience rather than shun certain strands of our theological history. I learned this way of doing ministry from a U.S. Army chaplain who studied liturgies and prayers in many traditions other than his own Muslim faith to make sure that he could serve soldiers of a variety of backgrounds while he was deployed at Guantanamo. To me, this demonstrated a true commitment to serve others. He helped me to reframe the core of our Unitarian Universalist commitment to diverse religious thought. It's one thing to say that we, as Unitarian Universalists, draw from many sources, including Jewish and Christian scriptures. But it is another thing to actually do it authentically and with deep respect for a variety of traditions.

Unitarian Universalism might grow more if we more fully embraced our principles of religious inclusivity. We tend to be religiously exclusive. We tend to ask our members to conform to our ways and preferences (not unlike the military). Unitarian Universalists frequently ask me if I struggle with being a Unitarian Universalist chaplain in the military. They imply that serving amid Christians is inherently problematic; that I may be shunned because of my religious identity. Or they assume that I have shunned Christianity, which I haven't, and therefore struggle to offer authentic Unitarian Universalist worship and ministry among Christians. At the heart of my ministry is a true dedication to help people practice the faith of their choosing using all the gifts at my disposal. To me that is the way to embrace our Principles and Purposes most fully.

My deployment to Iraq was a perfect example of carrying out an inclusive ministry. It was also an opportunity to learn about how other faiths need chaplains. I had substantial contact with Iraqis who had come to the hospital for medical treatment. There were women, children, and military detainees. The children often were brought in for burns they received due to the use of oil-burning stoves in their homes. We had so many children during one period that one physician, a pediatrician, seemed to be running her own pediatrics ward!

Having small children in a field hospital brought a different type of feeling and atmosphere. The staff, primarily accustomed to caring for soldiers and airmen who were injured or sick from duty, got a chance to relate in a different way with the younger patients. They displayed a new level of tenderness and caring. People who might not ordinarily come into the Intermediary Care Ward (ICW) stopped by to look at the children or visit with their mothers and fathers. The staff began soliciting specialty care packages for the kids. We needed baby blankets, toys, and other goodies to accommodate the families.

Because we had so many non-English speaking patients, there were contracted interpreters in the units, too. These persons were essential for doing ministry with local nationals. They helped me understand some things that I couldn't have figured out on my own. For example, our ICW had a TV-viewing and reading area for patients. Some of the programs were broadcast with Arabic subtitles for the Iraqis. But it turned out that many of them could not read, so the broadcasts were not as entertaining as initially conceived. The interpreters helped me develop a proposal for the Communications Squadron to begin a satellite service that had programming in the native languages, plus programming that was of greater interest. That felt like good ministry and the people seemed grateful.

It was also good ministry for the Air Force personnel, believe it or not. As the war drew to a close, there were fewer and fewer missions or things to do for the troops. Installing a new satellite was a project that gave them something meaningful to do for a few hours. It also afforded me the opportunity to establish new relationships with a unit that I ordinarily would not have crossed paths with. The military is all about relationships when it comes to getting stuff done. The more people you know, the more things you can make happen.

The interpreters also helped me understand that Muslims don't use chaplains or imams in the way Protestants typically do. I asked several detainees (usually combatants) if they wanted me to pray with them or wanted a Muslim clergyperson to visit them. Surprisingly, this was unheard of to them. Imams, I learned, do not visit people in the hospital or come to pray on behalf of others. The men typically prayed for themselves. What the detainees did need from me was help securing a *place* to pray. So we were able to arrange a few bed spaces in the ICW that we designated as for prayer only.

The detainees who could read also requested copies of the Qur'an. I learned that the military was distributing a religious text that we thought was the Qur'an but turned out to be just an interpretation of parts of the Qur'an. And it was in English. So I asked an interpreter to help me secure authentic copies of the Qur'an in Arabic, which he did. He had someone from off-base deliver several brand new copies that we could pass out to those who wanted to read the scriptures while awaiting treatment.

One of the oddest moments of interfaith ministry happened with an Army sergeant who visited the hospital frequently for physical therapy. She was at risk of being sent home due to an ankle injury. No one wants to go home before their unit is redeployed. I had a few visits with her to help her manage anxiety while in the hospital. Some of the visits occurred right there in the waiting area when no one else was in earshot. It turned out that she was Jewish. Since we didn't have a rabbi on the staff at the time, there was no opportunity for a Jewish service. But we did have some Jewish religious materials, including a menorah. It was stored deep in a chapel closet, not in use. So I loaned it to the sergeant with her promise to return it before she left. When I checked on her a couple weeks later, she had redeployed. The menorah was gone, too! I hope it is being put to good use.

Unitarian Universalist appreciation for faith formation in its many forms offers me a freedom that I want to take full advantage of. I embrace being the go-to chaplain for military members in the non-dominant faith groups. Military chaplains and chaplain assistants provide a unique service to members of the military and their families: We enable them to live out their faith commitments while they live out their obligation of defending the U.S. Constitution. No other military professionals can do this. We offer service members a place of solace and refuge. People come to chaplains when they have nowhere else to turn and no one else to whom they can entrust their most personal and sacred stories. This is a huge obligation.

I am delighted that the Unitarian Universalist Association has made significant strides recently in supporting military chaplaincy. The staff of the Ministries and Faith Development Department has raised the profile of military chaplains endorsed by the UUA in several ways. These include recognizing chaplains during the general sessions at General Assembly, hosting an annual retreat for military chaplains, and, in 2014, inviting one of our Army chaplains to preach during the Service of the Living Tradition. The retreat enables military chaplains, both currently serving and those in the pipeline, to gather for spiritual renewal, fellowship, and respite.

An ongoing challenge for Unitarian Universalists is learning how to embrace the military establishment and its service members, and to appreciate the military's role in preserving American religious freedoms, including the freedom of belief, worship, dissent, and interfaith dialogue. It would be a major step forward if a majority of Unitarian Universalists came to recognize that a standing military is essential for the free practice of religion. Without it, our constitutional freedoms would be severely jeopardized by encroaching nations. Military service members stand in the gap, to preserve the liberty enjoyed in our democratic republic.

Spirits Behind Bars

EMILY BRAULT

While the United States has only 5 percent of the world's population, it has 25 percent of the world's prisoners. In 2011, 1 in
every 107 adults in America was in jail or prison, and about 1 in
every 50 was on probation or parole, being supervised in their
community. One in 28 kids in the United States has a parent in
prison. For African-American kids, the number jumps to 1 in 9.

These statistics are publicized by the NAACP, the Pew Charitable Trusts, and even the Department of Justice. When religious
liberals hear about such things, our tendency is to do something about it. We are pragmatists and activists who organize for
reform and change. We learn about the causes, study the issues,
and work to transform society for the better. But sometimes we
miss the point. In a 1970 essay published in *Pastoral Care in the
Liberal Churches*, Unitarian Universalist minister Carl Wenner-
strom described how liberals might have acted at Calvary:

> The first liberal is there helping Jesus [carry the cross], but
> when the cross was placed in the ground and Jesus was
> nailed upon it, the liberal was not there. Perhaps he was off
> trying to get a stay of execution or a reversal of the convic-
> tion or planning for the future support of Jesus' family or the
> burial arrangements or getting up a petition to Rome on the
> irresponsibility of Pilate. The point is that he was absent at
> the point of the crucifixion—the time of personal suffering.

Sometimes we get so caught up in changing things for the better that we forget the significance, the fundamental importance, of being with people.

I work as a chaplain for the Oregon Department of Corrections. My office is next to the chapel in a medium/maximum security women's prison. On most days, it's a pretty depressing place. The building itself leaves much to be desired; concrete, echoing hallways painted a muted beige with no windows and little color. The chapel has some nice skylights, though, and carpeting. I think it's the nicest room in the place. And I only have to get buzzed through seven security doors to get there.

The women I work with are sentenced to anywhere from a year to life, some with and some without the possibility of parole. Can you imagine living the rest of your life in this place? Their yard is small and has no grass. There is no gym for basketball or other games when it is raining. They do have a workout room, which is about the size of a classroom and has a TV and DVD player for yoga or Zumba workouts when they have time. The rest of their days are pretty much like ours—they work or go to school, have medical and dental appointments, talk to their families and friends on the phone (the lucky ones get visits, and it's surprising how many of them don't), write and receive letters, listen to music, watch TV, and see their counselors, and some go to religious services. The difference is that all of these activities take place within one building the size of a small high school, surrounded by barbed wire and suffused by weird power dynamics.

The stereotype, of course, is that "bad" people go to prison. The reality is much more nuanced. Most of the women here made horrible choices that hurt a number of people, and our response as a society is to separate them from their communities and make them live here. Some of them continue to behave like jerks in prison; they fight or intimidate others, deal or use drugs, prey on the more vulnerable, lie and con and manipulate their way through the system. These are the 10 percent of the people that proverbially take up 90 percent of the staff's time. I find that most of the women, though, are trying to figure out how they ended up here and what they need to do to get out and stay out. With some learning and reflection and opportunity, the majority of them do just that. Eventually.

In the meantime, while they are in prison, they are stuck with me as their chaplain. My job is to provide for the religious and spiritual needs of the community as best I can. Practically speaking, that means I work with volunteers from a variety of faith traditions, scheduling their services and helping them adapt to the nuances of prison culture, and I provide direct counseling and care to adults in custody. A typical day might look something like this.

This morning I get a death notification before I even reach my office. Someone's mother died this morning. When I tell her, she tries really hard not to cry. "Not here," she insists. "It's not safe." But now is your chance! Get it out now before you go back to your unit! But no, she tries to suck her tears back into her body before they fall, like someone trying frantically to staunch a bleeding wound.

When she leaves, a captain comes in with more news. An inmate who was released seven days ago was hit by a car last night and died early this morning. Her sister is still here, and she has already been told. The grief and the fear run through everyone, though. She was well known, she was just released, she changed so much, she was doing so well! Later in the day the sister gets a card in the mail that says, "I'm doing great! I got to see my grandson for the first time! I'll send you pictures and keep in touch!" It is so sad.

After lunch I get a call from the mental health infirmary. A woman who is refusing her medications wants to talk to me. She has AIDS and asks questions like "Am I committing suicide if I don't take my meds? Am I saved? What's heaven like?" She had a chaplain at the county jail who had all the answers for her, told her what she needed to do, told her how to get saved. I'm not that kind of chaplain, I say. You need to find *your* answers, this is *your* journey. (Not the best response, in retrospect, but it's what comes out of my mouth at the moment.) Behind her questions is a need to be reassured: "Am I going to be okay?" God, I hope so—I give her that. She is saved. God loves her, even though it doesn't feel like it right now. She wants to die so badly, there is so much hurt and pain, this life is hell. And she wants to die soon. It is not happening quickly enough for her. I listen. And because I believe in life, I say, "Maybe there is a reason why you are still here. Maybe God still has plans for you here, things for you to do." She disagrees. When she winds down, I ask if she wants a prayer, and I pray for comfort and hope and courage. "I'll come by and see you again later this week, okay? We can talk some more?" She agrees.

I answer emails and phone calls from volunteers, staff, family members, and the like. I schedule a sweat lodge ceremony for this weekend and turn in paperwork for the Buddhist retreat next month. The Christians are having a baptism next week, so I need to arrange for the hose and the towels and the like to arrive on time and without incident. I make some photocopies for the Asatru group.

An officer sends someone down who got some bad news over the phone. She shows up sobbing at my door. Her kids were removed from their foster home because they were being sexually abused by one of the adults. "Are they going to be okay? What can I do?" She feels helpless and far away from them. What can any of us do? I listen. I agree that this sucks, that her pain makes sense, and I offer what I can to assure her she'll get through this. "I'm here if you need me." I say that line a lot. And I offer to pray. For comfort and hope and courage.

Some days the suffering is overwhelming. It's trapped inside the concrete walls and has nowhere else to go. It's in the water, the air, the lives that we live and the things that we do to each other and ourselves. It's in our minds and hearts, in the blood in our veins. We are so broken.

In *Understanding and Counseling Persons with Alcohol, Drug, and Behavioral Addictions* Howard Clinebell, one of my favorite writers on pastoral care and counseling, says, "For many people . . . life is like one long surgical operation without benefit of anesthesia." This is doubly true in prison. Not only are the lives of many of the people who end up here sadly messed up, our bureaucratic criminal justice system is broken and ineffective on many levels. It does include many great people with big hearts and the desire to help and serve and do the right thing!

But it is a system, a large one, that takes years to change and, in my humble opinion, is about twenty years behind the latest research on effective rehabilitation. Some states are better than others. Some prisons are better than others. I'm lucky to work in a prison system that is relatively educated, effective, and honorable. But on the whole, we are dealing with broken people in a broken system. It can be overwhelming at times.

In light of all this suffering and madness, I often feel like there is little I can do. Sure, I can hang out and practice the "ministry of presence" that I learned in my days of Clinical Pastoral Education (CPE), but I cannot change your sentence, diagnosis, or living situation. I can treat you with respect and dignity, but I cannot change your interactions with that officer who is burned out from too much forced overtime and not enough training. I can offer my skills in times of grief and loss, even crisis, but I cannot change the fact that you are locked in a twelve-by-six-foot cell twenty-three hours a day with a roommate who never sleeps or shuts up. I can pray with you, advocate for you, and argue that we should all treat one another more humanely, but I cannot take away your pain, fix your life, or make people treat you better. I cannot change the rules. I cannot change the system. I can only be here, a person offering love and light in a very dark place. And I have to know somewhere in the depths of my soul that it is enough.

One day last week I went and walked around the units a bit. I like to touch base with people outside of my office, just to say hi, check up on them. The dayrooms in the units all look out onto the yards, and in one of them a woman was dancing. She had headphones on, and she was skootching around the basketball court, dancing across to the weight pile, dancing as she walked, swinging her arms, rhythm in her step, spinning. I watched her from the dayroom, through the windows, as she spun and sang, high-stepping around the yard. I asked a woman next to me, "Do you know who she is?"

She said, "I can't think of her name, but she's the one who waves as the trains go by, too."

"Good for her," I said. "Good for her." Here on this overcast, chilly day, surrounded by concrete and barbed wire, dressed in prison blues but with her headphones in her ears and her heart in her feet, she had found something good. A little joy, perhaps. A little light. I hope I can do that, too.

There are a few particular skills that you need in this work, but for the most part, being a representative of love, and the sacred, and community is surprisingly effective. It's surprising how much healing takes place when you just listen to people, hearing their stories and acknowledging their lives. It helps if you are well versed in grief, loss, and crisis care. You need to be aware of con games and how to avoid being set up; if you have an internal bullshit meter, bring it along. A working knowledge of addiction, mental illness, and criminal thinking patterns is helpful, as well as pastoral counseling approaches to them. You need to build relationships with both staff and inmates, or you won't be effective with either. You need good boundaries. Being quick on your feet comes in handy as well. You need to have a deep well of spiritual practice, self-awareness, and self-care, because the negativity is overwhelming. But most importantly, you need to show up. If you are grounded in the big love, others will benefit just by your being there. As the Gospel of Phillip, one of the gnostic Gospels, says,

> Spiritual love is wine and fragrance. All those who anoint themselves with it take pleasure in it. While those who are anointed are present, those nearby also profit from the fragrance. If those anointed with ointment withdraw from them and leave, then those not anointed, who merely stand nearby, still remain in their bad odor.
>
> The Samaritan gave nothing but wine and oil to the wounded man. It is nothing other than the ointment. It healed the wounds, for "love covers a multitude of sins" [1 Peter 4:8].

This passage reminds me of a conversation I had once with a staff member at a juvenile facility in Minnesota. I was describing an exchange that I had had with a member of my church, in which I was encouraging him to consider mentoring one of our kids in custody. His response was something along the lines of

"Oh, no, not me. Those kids need someone who can relate to them better, who shares their experiences in life." To which the staff member responded, "Well, that's ridiculous. The kid just wants someone to love him."

The ironic thing is that every time I preach at a Unitarian Universalist church about my work, at least one person from the congregation approaches me afterward with a story of a family member who was or is in prison. At first this surprised me, as I had bought into the illusion that prison was for others, not us. As a group we are primarily white, educated, and financially stable, and have better access to social resources that many others in our country. Never mind that my own father did time in prison (and he happened to be a county court judge when he fell). I somehow made it through seminary and some excellent pastoral training without shedding my assumption that I was going to work with Them, and that my tradition, my church, provided me with an Us to come home to! It was as though I were a missionary or something—off to work in a foreign land, trying to bridge two worlds with love and learning and all good things. Ha! Then I was reminded that my community is in prison, too. Thank the gods for that! My dad, your daughter, our brothers and uncles and friends. How could it be otherwise? The rain falls on us all, and we are not immune to any of the brokenness that life has to offer.

Living in the truth that my family is in prison brings passion to my work more than any other idea or theology or experience. It challenges me, annoys me, and requires me to wrestle with the meaning and purpose of pain, abuse, suffering, madness, and healing. Or maybe it pushes me to get beyond the meaning and purpose, and to find that field that Rumi talks about:

Out beyond ideas of wrongdoing and rightdoing,
there is a field. I'll meet you there.
When the soul lies down in that grass,
the world is too full to talk about.
Ideas, language, even the phrase *each other*
doesn't make any sense.

It requires me to choose love, and some days I'm not really sure what that looks like.

One of the ways I practice love is by remembering. By *remembering* I mean not nostalgic reminiscences of the past, or something we do with our brains, but *re-membering*: returning people to membership, or bringing people into community, or something we do with our hearts and our guts. People in prison are often a forgotten people. Many of them are cut off from their families. They have been removed from their communities. They are known primarily for the most awful things they have done, and the rest of their humanity is generally discounted as irrelevant to what they "deserve." When I remember people, when I build relationship and community with them, I am acknowledging the actuality of their life and affirming the worth and dignity of their existence. I am listening to their stories, and I am experiencing them as people, as children of God. They might be really messed-up children of God, but still, they are family. They are our brothers and sisters, our moms and dads, and our children. When we remember them, we bring them (back) into the membership of community. They are a part of us, and we are a part of them. As Martin Luther King Jr. said in his sermon "On Being A Good Neighbor," "In the final analysis, I must not ignore the wounded man on life's Jericho Road, because he is a part of me and I am a part of him. His agony diminishes me, and his salvation enlarges me."

One of the side effects of remembering, of bringing people into community, is that we are changed. That's one of the reasons it's so hard to reach out beyond what we already know, beyond our comfort zones: because it changes us. Think of your own experiences. Maybe you have experiences of abuse, addiction, or poverty. As you bring them into your consciousness and face them and process them and integrate them into your life, you are changed. The way you relate to people changes. The way you relate to yourself changes. To put it more bluntly, experiences of addiction transform the way you deal with stress or grief or loneliness. Experiences of poverty affect your relationship with money and economic situations. Experiences of abuse transform the ways you relate to people. You can no longer live like you used to. You are a different person. You see things differently. You experience things differently.

In religious parlance, these experiences are, in fact, prophetic. They challenge the life that we have (or think we have), and everything changes. Sometimes they turn our world upside down. Abuse happens, trauma happens, and now we have to reimagine our lives, maybe even re-evaluate our lives, and learn to live in a different way. That's downright subversive! Those experiences are dangerous!

For example, here we have our little circle of life, with our traditions, experiences, and assumptions sitting right in the middle. One of my favorite assumptions is, "Just relax, it'll work itself out." But I would guess that for most people this isn't true. "Just relax, it'll work itself out." Despair continues. Depression continues. Mental illness continues. "Just wait it out, it'll work itself out." Poverty continues. Abuse continues. "It'll work itself out." Economic despair continues. Oppression continues . . . prejudice . . . discrimination. When we take these experiences from the margins, whether they are people, ideas, or societies, and remember them into our circle, the assumption, "It'll work itself out" doesn't work anymore. There is a new light shed on the topic, and we begin to see things as we never have before. Our vision is different now. We are larger than we used to be. We see farther and experience more. When we remember these dangerous memories, we live out the fulfillment of what it means to be a faithful community.

The healing power of remembering, of leaning into the big love, is not only that we are challenged to live out our commitment to love, and to care, and to remember, but also that other people gain the opportunity to choose their life.

Here's an example. When I was about ten years old I was running amuck. I was a child of a single mom who worked full time and did a good job of putting a roof over our heads and taking care of me. But I was out stealing stuff and getting into fights and causing mayhem in the community. We happened to live not far away from my great-aunt and great-uncle, Florence and Dale, and one day Florence called up my mom and said, "We would like to take Emily on Wednesday nights." My mom

must have said, "Woo-hoo!" So every Wednesday after school
I would go over to Aunt Florence and Uncle Dale's. Since I was
ten years old at the time, my great-aunt and great-uncle were
maybe a hundred and forty in my mind. Florence would show
me the quilt she was working on or the flowers in her garden.
I wasn't very interested in quilts or flowers, but she wanted to
show me—she wanted to share this with me, and so she did.
When Uncle Dale got home from work we would shoot hoops
or play pool, and he would always have jokes tucked in his
pocket that he took from *Boys' Life* or some such magazine at
work, and he would share those with me. For dinner Florence
would doctor up some of those little Totino's pizzas, the ones
that you could get five for a quarter, and gather up radishes
from the garden, and Florence and Dale would have their cup
of hot water with lemon, and I would have my milk. When we
were done we would go off to church. They would go to choir
practice and I would go to whatever kids' group was going on
at the time. When that was done they would drive me home.
Every Wednesday it was the same. Every Wednesday. The same.

Understand that we didn't have much in common. My life
was very different from theirs. We ran in different economic,
social, moral, and religious circles. Yet they chose me. They
reached out to me. They welcomed me into their home. They
shared their life with me. And they were interested in my life
in return. It made me think, "Well, if they are so interested in
my life, maybe my life is worth being interested in after all.
Maybe I do have something inside me that is worth spending
time with, and hanging out with, and getting to know." I was
re-membered. I was seen. And because I was seen, I could start
seeing myself as well.

When I talk about the importance of relationships, the
importance of remembering, I'm not talking about enmeshed,
co-dependent, mushy feel-good relationships that make everybody feel warm and fuzzy inside. That's not what I'm talking
about. True relationships have to acknowledge that there is an
in-between. I am me, and you are you. I have my experiences,
perspectives, and ways of being in the world, and you have
yours, and there is an in-between (that sometimes looks like

a gulf) that we must intentionally choose to bridge. We must deliberately choose to love. We must actively choose to participate in the lives of other people. We must do this not because we are enmeshed and co-dependent, but because of the reality of our experiences and our connections to one another. Otherwise, we'll be stuck in our little tiny worlds and never learn a thing about our potential to love.

Besides not always feeling mushy and comfortable, these relationships are also not going to be perfect, nor should they be. It's like the Leonard Cohen song "Anthem" says:

Forget your perfect offering.
There is a crack in everything.
That's how the light gets in.

Forget your perfect relationships and perfect community, forget about having your life all together, having your memories all figured out and incorporated into your life, there is a crack in everything and that's how the light gets in. It is through our imperfections, it is through our goofs and gaffes and incomplete abilities, bound by our intention, that the light of humanity, grace, and love truly gets in.

Our spirits are behind bars. We are locked up and locked down when we forget to show up at the time of crucifixion, when we forget that life is difficult and we need to be there. We need to remember, and to be remembered. One of my favorite hymns in the Unitarian Universalist hymnal is "Come, Sing a Song with Me" by Carolyn McDade:

Come, sing a song with me
that I might know your mind.

Not that I might change your mind. Not that I might fix your mind or convert your mind or give answers to your mind, but that I might know your mind. The hymn continues:

And I'll bring you hope
when hope is hard to find.

And I'll bring a song of love
and a rose in the wintertime.

Just by knowing you, by singing with you and being with
you and spending time with you, I will bring you hope When
things are dark and dreary and the days are short and the nights
are long, and the sky is gray and cold, singing with you and
knowing you, *remembering you*, will bring you hope and love
and add a little color to your day. I'm not bringing you all the
answers. I'm not bringing you knowledge or wisdom or solutions, I'm bringing you a rose in the wintertime, some color in
the bleakness, some warmth in the cold.

Come, walk in rain with me
that I might know your mind.

I live in Oregon. This is a given. We will get wet, our mascara
will run and our hair will get messy and we won't look pretty,
but I want to know your mind.

Also note that this is not a one-time request. The song
implores each request three times: "Come, dream a dream with
me; come, dream a dream with me; come, dream a dream with
me . . ." If at first you don't succeed, try, try again. There is a
certain stubbornness here, a certain persistence in the effort to
build that bridge and remember one another.

The central act of caring, of ministry, is being in relationship.
Ministry does not mean fixing people or saving people. It does
not mean rescuing people from their lives. It means hearing and
seeing and remembering in relationships. This is an affront to
the idea that we need to save the world, and a call instead to
enter into a relationship of care and compassion because that
is when the power of salvation, of grace and love and reunion,
shines through. We must sing songs with each other. Not as
saviors, not as buoys, but as companions, as fellow humans on
this mysterious journey of life.

Together we are creating new experiences of the in-between,
of the power of relationship, of the light that comes in through
the cracks, and that is what brings hope and keeps us alive.

We are not trying to change one another, but we are trying to know one another, and we are changed in that experience. This, I believe, is our sacred task.

Coming to Wholeness

BARBARA E. STEVENS

The group room is large enough to hold twenty-five mis-matched chairs. Fluorescent lights supplement the thin glow that seeps through the windows on this rainy fall day in western Oregon. From where I stand in front of the whiteboard, I can see the row of maple trees planted out front and the spot where the residents smoke during their breaks. The highway hums in the background.

The residents in this hospital detoxification and stabilization unit sit facing me, the chaplain. They receive medical supervision while they come off alcohol, heroin and other opioids, or benzodiazepines, which are anti-anxiety medications they may have taken as prescribed or bought on the street. About half are in early stages of detox. They huddle in blankets, dazed, medicated with Valium. If they used methamphetamine, they're probably asleep. Those coming off opioids are restless, irritable, complaining of achy bones. Although the medication they receive takes away the worst of their pain, the opioid addicts still feel as if they have a bad flu. The ones detoxing from benzodiazepines experience a rebound effect, so the anxiety they stifled, perhaps for years, returns amplified. They can't sleep; they can't think.

Given all this, one may wonder why we bother leading groups. Lying in bed, however, with lots of time to think, is not helpful for our residents, and even when they feel miserable, they may hear something in a group that strikes them, or they may remember an activity. We never know what might make the difference for someone's sobriety. Besides, not all of them are miserable. The other half of the group have been here a week or so and are feeling a lot better. They encourage the newcomers, and they engage. I count on them to carry the group.

Today's group is about grief and loss. Toward the end of the hour, we may have time to talk about spirituality. I start the class by having them call out all the things they've lost in their addiction, and I write what they say on the board, dividing the list into the six categories of loss outlined by Kenneth Mitchell and Herbert Anderson in *All Our Losses, All Our Griefs*: relationship, functional, material, role, systemic, and intrapsychic.

They easily name enough losses to cover all the categories. Everyone's life is full of loss, and when you have an active addiction, the losses are multiplied. The residents have lost their health; they have seen friends die from drugs, accidents, and violence; they have had children taken away by the Department of Human Services; they have lost jobs, homes, cars, and sometimes everything they ever owned. They have suffered assaults on their self-esteem, on their person, on their dreams. Many of them feel broken, lonely, and scared. They may be left with nothing but the bit of hope that spurred them to enter treatment.

I feel blessed because I get to watch them begin to heal. As they sit with their peers and feel understood by those who've walked where they've walked, addicts[1] begin to open up. They discover that others care about what they have to say. Their peers encourage them, hug them, and then share their own pain. Maybe for the first time in their lives, these people are in an environment where it is okay to admit they hurt.

It may also be the first time in their lives when they haven't felt judged. The shame they experience can be overwhelming,

---

1   Throughout this chapter, I use the term "addict" to include the alcoholic, use the word "drug" to include alcohol (because alcohol is a drug), and use the words "sober" and "clean" interchangeably. Because I work with substance abusers, I focus on chemical dependency. Some behavioral addictions, such as to gambling or sex, can be as devastating as chemical addictions. Behavioral addicts need our understanding and empathy as much as substance abusers.

but I find it helpful to remember that none of them imagined, when they started using, that they would one day forsake everything they loved, betray their values, and destroy their bodies for a substance that eventually stopped giving them pleasure. Although a few hold on to fond memories of getting high, by the time they come to treatment most of them have stopped enjoying the drug and use it simply to keep from getting sick. Now they have the opportunity to get well.

At first, though, they don't feel as if they're getting well. Detoxification is a painful process. But no matter how they feel physically, while they are here they can engage with people like themselves. If they are open and eager to learn, they can grow an amazing amount in the two weeks they are with us.

Regardless of their eagerness, though, they probably don't feel comfortable talking about loss, and when we talk about spirituality, usually someone in the group feels angry or betrayed. When I first led these groups, residents would sometimes argue, swear at me, or walk out. Over the years, I have made adjustments, so now that rarely happens.

For instance, at the beginning of each group, I set some ground rules. I remind them we are going to talk in general terms, about ideas and strategies. We are not telling stories of our losses. Although I will sit with people in my office while they grieve, that is not the purpose of this group. These residents are too early in their recovery, too tender and vulnerable, to cope with the depth of pain and loss that fills the room. Most residents have lost something recently: maybe a marriage, a job, their health, a friend who became disabled from drug use, or a loved one who died. If we talk too much about the experience of loss, they become overwhelmed. And when addicts become overwhelmed, they are at risk of relapse.

I have similar ground rules for the spirituality discussion. Again, we talk about ideas, about what spirituality is and how it might support us in recovery. We don't talk about what we individually believe, and we certainly don't challenge anyone else's beliefs. As a Unitarian Universalist chaplain, I find it easy to honor a diversity of paths and beliefs. The residents often have a harder time doing so.

That is why I remind them that whatever someone else says, it has nothing to do with them. Don't take it personally, I tell them. No one is trying to discount what they think. One of the norms of the group is that "acceptance does not mean agreement." In other words, we can accept others without sharing their beliefs—especially their spiritual beliefs. As a Unitarian Universalist chaplain, I can model this acceptance.

No matter what I say, and no matter how cautious I am, however, some residents are so triggered by the word *spirituality*, or feel so private about their beliefs, that they are uncomfortable with this group. That is fine. I do not ask people to like the group; I do not even make them stay. I prefer to honor their emotions, express gratitude for whatever feedback they offer, and remain caring and calm. Some days this is easier for me than others. Yet if I tell the residents not to take things personally, I need to set an example.

An Addiction Chaplain's Day

This once-a-week group is only a small part of what I do as a chaplain for a residential treatment program. My work includes setting an example of calmness and kindness throughout the day, being a non-anxious presence, and being available to residents and staff if they need to talk. I lead a daily meditation, go on walks with the residents, and sit in the kitchen with them. As a member of the interdisciplinary team, I attend daily staff meetings, where I may advocate for the patients, remind staff of patients' stories to enhance their empathy, or raise issues the others might not have had time to notice. During most of my day, however, I meet individually with residents in my office.

Residents talk to me about their shame and guilt, or about the abuse they suffered and the resentment they feel. They wonder how they can ever forgive parents, ex-lovers, or the system. Most of them have deep grief over losses they never faced, so we talk about people who have died, children they wish they had been there for, homes, jobs, health, and the self they lost to a lifestyle they could not control. Because I don't have time to meet with everyone, and not every resident wants to open up to me anyway, I started the group on loss to introduce them to basic ideas of grief and help them figure out how they can begin mourning the many losses of their lives.

Exactly why I feel drawn to work with this population, however, and why I am able to care about them in spite of their lies, manipulations, and emotional outbursts, I am not sure. When I went into chaplaincy, I originally intended to work with people who had major mental illnesses, because there is mental illness in my family of origin. Addiction is considered a mental illness, of course, and many people on our unit have a co-occurring mental health diagnosis, but I never expected to work with addicts. Indeed, before doing my Clinical Pastoral Education (CPE), I didn't know much about addiction. When my residency supervisor placed me in the substance abuse program, however, I discovered I was in my element.

Quite simply, I love the people I work with. Compassion for them comes easily to me. Some days are harder than others, of course, and some people are hard for me to like. To remain nonjudgmental, open, and compassionate, I depend on my Unitarian Universalist values and my relationship with my own higher power. Along with my spiritual practice, which includes prayer, meditation, reflection, and a connection with nature, I gain strength and hope from my faith tradition, which honors the wisdom of science, prophetic men and women, and all the world's religions.

Because science and reason help me understand how the brain works and teach me about the interaction between genetic predisposition and upbringing, I can't be certain that, if I were in the same situation as the residents, I would behave more nobly. I also believe, on the basis of recent scientific insights and teachings from the world's mystical traditions, that not only is everything interdependent, but everything is one. There is no separation between myself and others.

Thus the man who stole from his parents, the woman who abandoned her child, the addict who betrayed her friend to get money for drugs, the alcoholic who doesn't understand how his drinking hurt his family, and the woman who prostituted herself are, underneath everything, no different than I am. The man who won't talk to me because I don't preach Jesus, the older woman who compliments me because she wants something from me, the young man who tells me the voice I use during meditation enrages him, and even the dealer who checked into the unit because he thought it would be a great place to find new customers are all me. I am them.

So how can I judge them? If, like them, I panicked and started shouting, or betrayed all the values I was taught, I hope someone would recognize the fear and hurt beneath my behavior and speak to that. I hope someone would listen to me, model calmness and faith, and invite me to behave with dignity, integrity, and courage.

So this is what I try to do for them.

There But for Grace

Having been raised Unitarian Universalist, I have a tendency to believe my rational mind can solve my problems. As a white American woman, raised in a middle-class household, I sometimes forget that I succeed not just because of my own efforts, but also because of what I learned as a child, who I grew up knowing, and how I look. I sometimes forget that I stand on the backs not only of my ancestors who were educated professionals, but also of generations of servants and nurses and construction workers whose labor and care allowed me to thrive.

Sometimes I think I earned the ease of my life. Not that my life has been always easy. I have dealt with deaths, financial insecurity, and illness. Nonetheless, I own a home and two cars. I am happily married. I speak English and know how to navigate government systems. I can hire an accountant and see a doctor when I need to.

I suspect this is true for many Unitarian Universalists who tend to think that hard work is rewarded. Even though on some level we know better, we may think we control the events in our lives, as if catastrophe does not happen to us. And if we were raised with enough financial abundance and social supports, we may take them for granted.

If no disaster gets in our way, we may die feeling we earned the gifts we received. And certainly, most of us do work hard, care about others, and give to charitable causes. We are good people. Don't we deserve a comfortable life?

Of course we do. So does everyone else. Yes, everyone. Even the lazy, the evil, the greedy, the rich, the untouchable. We all deserve to live in peace, without suffering, to know we are loved, and to feel hope. The universe offers no such guarantee, of course, and a pain-free life probably wouldn't be good for us, anyway. Suffering and adversity give us the opportunity to grow—assuming our lives haven't been filled with trauma after trauma, and assuming we have someone who loves us and can guide us to recovery. Over the years, I've noticed that people who've had relatively stable lives do well in recovery. Some even stay sober on their own. The addicts who end up on our unit, on the other hand, have endured a lifetime of abuse and abandonment. Some have few memories of love and support.

Perhaps you've lived through horrible traumas. Maybe you endured childhood abuse, or your son was murdered, or you were raped or kidnapped, or your home was destroyed by an earthquake. If so, you probably understand how life can leave us adrift, terrified, isolated, enraged, hopeless. Maybe you understand how, if we don't have loved ones to nurture us, we could turn to drugs to survive.

You don't have to endure extreme suffering to empathize, however. We are all human. To some degree, we've all experienced love, loss, betrayal, hope, and abandonment. We relate to one another not because our stories are the same, but because we have experienced the same emotions. That's what I discovered. Through spiritual practice, writing, counseling, spiritual direction, and CPE, I learned to face and tolerate those feelings within myself, so now, as a chaplain, I can listen without my fears and sadness getting in the way. I can hold a sacred space of openness and love for the people I serve.

The Work of Love

At times, my ability to do this has been tested, as with the sex offender who wanted forgiveness, or the man who brought drugs onto the unit and shot up a young woman who had never before used a needle. We humans sometimes do terrible things to one another. My Unitarian Universalist values, my human values, inform me that this is wrong. They also inform me that, while I do not have the power to forgive people for the hurts they've done to others, I can speak to the power of forgiveness and the importance of making amends. I can also remember that God loves both the abused and the abuser, even if the abuser never acknowledges what they have done. Therefore, no matter who I'm working with or what they tell me, I am called to love them.

Love does not mean just acceptance and forgiveness; it also means holding people accountable. This may not be so true on a cancer or cardiovascular unit, even though cancer and heart disease are made more likely by certain behaviors, but it definitely is when working with addicts. For me to effectively challenge someone, however, I must first develop a relationship with them. I must first accept them. Then they will respond better when I say, "Wow, you sure got angry over that little thing," or "I wonder what your part was in that," or "I hear you want to leave. What's going on?"

But not everyone, especially in early recovery, is ready to think about how they created their own misery, so my first task is to affirm. After I have honored a resident's suffering, I might probe a bit to see how they will respond if I lift up inconsistencies in what they said, or reflect their words back so they can see how unlikely they sound. If a resident has hurt others, and feels guilt and shame, I will acknowledge that, yes, they did wrong, perhaps grave wrong. They can't take it back, and that's sad.

At the same time, I stay with them. I do not cringe or show disgust. I sit with them while they grieve, or don't, and I love them through it all. I do this because the love simply arises within me, but also because my values tell me that love is the most important gift I can offer, and because I know that we are so much more than just our guilty deeds and resentments. I also know that when we shame ourselves, we tend to relapse. During early recovery, we need to focus on healing. In the twelve-step program, acknowledging the harm we have done comes after we find something larger than ourselves to turn to for support. Making amends comes even later.

Given this, a Unitarian Universalist chaplain has a lot to offer people for healing. Our hesitance to acknowledge sin can leave us without a good way to talk about evil, and yet the Universalist value of eternal love is powerful. This love is given to all, simply because we exist. The love of Universalism claims even the most despicable person, embracing the purity of whatever is left of their soul and touching their brokenness and scars with a transformative, healing power.

It can be hard to see the divinity in some people, however. I have sat with residents who seemed to have no soul, no heart, no open place for me to probe. They talked to me because they wanted some special privilege they thought I could give. At such times, I feel as empty as the person in front of me. Love seems a long way off.

Still, my Unitarian Universalist values remind me that the power of love is greater than the power of evil, and that mystery is as valid as science and reason. So even if I don't experience that Universalist love in that moment, I believe that love is in the room, and I pray to it for help staying respectful, compassionate, and kind. My Unitarian Universalist values also remind me of the importance of justice and the beloved community, so I insist that the resident be respectful, as well. Accountability is part of love, and accepting responsibility is one way we resolve our shame.

Therefore, no matter who the residents are or what they've done, I give them as much time as they want to meet with me. I remain gentle and respectful, even when they get angry or irrational. When I remind them of the rules or encourage them to act with kindness, I do so because I believe in them: I believe they are capable of learning to love.

A Piece of the Truth

Sometimes residents are not ready to love, either themselves or others. Maybe they feel too empty, angry, lonely, scared. Maybe they're not ready to face themselves, and they start using again. In such situations, I have felt angry, and I have been moved to tears. Nonetheless, my Unitarian Universalist values remind me that I don't know everything. I may have a piece of the truth, but I don't have it all. So although I want the residents to stay clean and sober, to engage in meaningful work, to find love, I don't know the true meaning of life. I don't know what another person's path should be. I don't even know what is in the best interest of all concerned. Eventually, all the residents I have loved will leave the unit. I must release them to the higher power that is theirs.

This acceptance may seem antithetical to our Unitarian Universalist passion for justice, equity, fairness, and the democratic process. When residents tell me about the abuse they suffered as children, or formerly incarcerated residents share how difficult it is for them to find a job or an apartment, or homeless residents talk about their struggles, I may notice anger rise within me. I want the world to be fair; I want to eradicate bigotry and hatred.

My anger, however, does not help the residents. Not only does it take attention away from them and put it onto my feelings, but my emotion may be misplaced. Addicts are notorious for manipulating people and blaming others for their problems.

Of course, injustice is real. Systems abuse people; people abuse people. Healing is needed. Many residents want to learn to navigate bureaucracies, or expunge their felony convictions, or join groups that are trying to change the world. So I research resources and offer practical suggestions.

But I'm a chaplain, not a social worker or an activist. My main work is to be present, to listen with compassion, to honor residents, to lift up the sacred within each soul, and to believe in each one. My Unitarian Universalist beliefs and values help me do that.

Some of what helps me hold steady in the face of residents who daily confront and afflict me, though, has nothing to do with Unitarian Universalism. For instance, I feel compassion when I get to know residents through their stories. I imagine what it's like to feel physically miserable and be stuck inside a building with little freedom for most of the day, and I empathize. And I remember that addiction is a disease.

Being "Normal"

Is addiction really a disease? Isn't that an excuse? If addicts had enough willpower, wouldn't they just stop using?

These are controversial questions. Putting a substance in our body is, on some level, a choice, so many people believe addiction is a moral failing. A mother who abandons her child when she relapses on heroin isn't sick, they reason; she's sinful. Some addicts choose recovery even when they're struggling with horrific challenges, so shouldn't they all be able to?

Perhaps. But we used to think that people with schizophrenia, major depression, or bipolar disorder had demons inside them. As we better understand the brain, we realize we are born with quirks and disorders that influence who we are, how we perceive the world, and what choices we make. Some studies show that addiction runs in families, not just because of how we are raised, but also because of genetics.[2]

What really helped me understand the intractability of addiction, however, was a chart on the website of the National Institute on Drug Abuse (published in *Drugs, Brain, and Behavior: The Science of Addiction*) showing that the rate of relapse for addicts is about the same as that for people with diabetes, hypertension, and asthma. Addicts are not the only ones whose "weakness" gets in the way of their taking care of themselves or who can't control their impulses. If we're born with certain propensities toward behavioral or physical difficulties, or we grow

---

2   Useful resources include Dean Hamer and Peter Copeland, *Living with Our Genes: Why They Matter More Than You Think*; David J. Linden, *The Compass of Pleasure: How Our Brains Make Fatty Foods, Orgasm, Exercise, Marijuana, Generosity, Vodka, Learning, and Gambling Feel So Good*; Gabor Mate, *In the Realm of the Hungry Ghosts: Close Encounters with Addiction*; *Pleasure Unwoven*, a video available from the Institute for Addiction Study (www.institute foraddictionstudy.com); and the websites of the Substance Abuse and Mental Health Services Administration (www.samhsa.gov) and the National Institute on Drug Abuse (www.drugabuse.gov). The CDC offers information about the connections between adverse childhood experiences (ACEs) and later addiction and incarceration at www.cdc.gov/violenceprevention/acestudy/. For a discussion of how shame feeds addiction, read the work of John Bradshaw to understand the addict and Melodie Beatty to understand the person whose life revolves around the addict, the "codependent."

up in chaotic families that exacerbate those natural tendencies, we will make bad choices and mess up our lives, even if we don't do so with drugs. I experienced a fair amount of stability and a lot of love as a child, yet I sometimes lose control of my emotions. How can I expect people whose lives have been chaotic since they were born, who may never have been taught to be kind or vulnerable or respectful, to do a good job of managing theirs?

In therapeutic circles, we talk about the benefits people get from acting out, and it is also true that some people have been taught to be victimized for so long, they don't know how to be anything but a victim. Other residents spend most of their time manipulating others. Yet most of them want to live differently. They don't want to keep acting out. They want to be "normal."

We Unitarian Universalists may have trouble understanding this desire to be normal. I, for instance, was taught to look down on the "normal" person. Unitarianism in particular has historically honored the individual, the renegade, the heretic. We talk about positive thinking and creating our own reality. But this is a feel-good theology that doesn't mean much to those living in poverty or war zones, where children go hungry and mothers cry themselves to sleep and there's no guarantee you'll make it alive to school, if there even is a school for you. Breathing exercises and mindfulness don't make the peeling paint look any better or the broken toilet flush. When your world is like that, when your parents are addicts, when you've never felt at home in your body, that first sip of alcohol or first hit of marijuana can change everything. Suddenly, you have no more problems: You don't care how many men your mother brings home or if your father ever makes it to one of your basketball games, and your social anxiety is gone.

In Cheryl Strayed's book *Tiny Beautiful Things*, a collection of letters to her "Dear Sugar" advice column, one writer offers this description of normal: "Normality means no one is screaming, fighting, or insulting one another. Normality means I'm not sobbing in my room. Normality means Christmas and other family holidays are a joy."

This is the kind of normal we would all want.

The Challenges and Gifts of Projections

No matter how abnormal our lives have been, and no matter how much we share a longing for normality instead, our chaplaincy is most effective if we keep our feelings and thoughts out of the way. Just because we've suffered doesn't mean we know what it's like for someone else to suffer. We need to listen to their story without getting caught up in our own. That doesn't mean our story won't ever come up. But if we've explored our insecurities, our pain and suffering, our fear and rage, we won't often be caught unaware by them. Addicts can be volatile, frightened, and lonely, and they can trigger fear and sadness in us. Their projections and transference will bring up our own. Recognizing our countertransference will help us stay clear and open.

Staying clear and open also helps when residents project their feelings onto us. No matter what kind of chaplaincy we do, our role brings up expectations in others. Residents may be nervous around me because they fear I will try to bring them to Jesus, or they may be disappointed because I don't seek converts, or they'll ask me to pray with them because that's the only way they know to get my attention, or they won't like me because I remind them of their mother.

So I invite them to tell me more, or I chat with them on walks, or I ask them to teach me what they know about God. Through these interactions, most residents decide I'm not so scary after all, and maybe next time they come across someone who seems different, they'll be more open.

One resident was angry at me because I symbolized for him an entire generation, all the Baby Boomers who had sold out, voted for Reagan, and left the Gen-Xers with a mess. There was truth in this. We Boomers have created an economic, social, and environmental mess. Yet gentle exploration yielded a deeper truth: The resident's anger wasn't just at me and my generation. It was also at having been let down by his Baby Boomer parents. As he examined his resentment toward them, he found a way to forgive them. With his anger softened, he realized his experiences had given him a passion for justice that he no longer had to cover up by getting loaded. Instead, he could use that passion to create a better world.

If my gray hair had not brought up his anger, none of that healing would have been possible. In such ways, projections can be gifts.

Back to the Group

But on the day that I'm leading group, I can sense the residents have had enough of talking about loss, so we move on. We do a brainstorm on the words *religion* and *spirituality*. Because the deeply religious can feel disenfranchised in this exercise, I remind the group not to take personally what anyone says. A brainstorm includes anything that comes to a person's mind; it doesn't mean they believe what they've said. I find that such reminders help when talking about a topic as emotional as religion, as does setting limits on faith statements.

As the brainstorm progresses, it's clear that this group has more positive things to say about religion than most. Still, the exercise lets some of them get out the negative associations they have with it, such as sexual abuse and war. This helps them let go of that "bad" god. The brainstorm on the word *spirituality* can then help them replace that negative image of the sacred with a healthy one.

As we complete the activity, this group defines spirituality as something serene, loving, mystical; that is found in nature, in us, in connections; and that gives us hope and strength. I explain that the root of the word *spirituality* is *spiritus*, which means breath. Spirituality, I tell them, is anything that gives life or is life-affirming.

As a Unitarian Universalist, however, I don't expect the residents to accept my definition of spirituality. They need to find their own. Through this exercise, I hope they've come to their own understanding of spirituality, maybe even re-envisioned their faith or thought about a higher power in a different way, a way that can help them stay sober. If I can help shatter their painful and limiting images of God and instead offer them a god who is kind and wise, I will be grateful. For recovery is hard enough; we don't need to try to recover alone.

In this way, the class comes to an end. We haven't finished the work of freeing God, and some residents are still confused about the topic, but we have made a start. Anyone who wants to talk further can do so with me in private.

But even residents who have found a loving, supportive higher power probably still need to free themselves. Most addicts, for instance, benefit from counseling to deal with the traumas and losses they've endured. Following a twelve-step program may help, as may many cognitive behavioral strategies, or meditation and other practices. In this way, little by little, they learn to let go of resentments, to forgive themselves and others, and to not only love, but accept being loved themselves. Little by little, they learn to trust.

Faith and Trust

Trust is vital. Although faith is not synonymous with trust, the two concepts are similar. Meher Baba, in his *Discourses*, writes about the importance of three types of faith for a healthy spiritual life: faith in oneself; faith in "the Master"; and faith in life itself. He says we have to trust in these three faiths to find peace, connection, and wholeness.

Many of the residents who come through our unit have lost faith in all those areas. Of course, giving everything over to God does not solve all our problems. We still have a lot of work to do if we're going to stay clean and sober. Gerald G. May points this out in his book *Addiction and Grace*. Neither "turning everything over to divine will" nor depending solely on our own will can keep us sober. "Instead, *the power of grace flows most fully when human will chooses to act in harmony with divine will.* In practical terms, this means staying in a situation, being willing to confront it as it is, remaining responsible for the choices one makes in response to it, but at the same time turning to God's grace, protection, and guidance as the ground for one's choices and behavior."

Ultimately, this is what I strive to help the residents do: stay with their feelings, confront what must be confronted, accept responsibility for themselves and their choices, and find a higher power that can walk with them in all they do, to whom they can turn when they feel overwhelmed, who loves them completely and will never abandon them, even if they relapse.

Because my Unitarian Universalist tradition is open to any uplifting, life-affirming faith, I can celebrate their belief in Jesus Christ, Kali, Allah, or the Goddess. Because I know I don't have all the truth, I'm comfortable in the not-knowing, so I can help residents feel comfortable with not knowing as well.

Trust and comfort with uncertainty does not happen in an hour or overnight. When they sit with me and share their lives and dreams, the residents start to trust: They trust me to be careful with their stories and their souls. If I betray that trust, I set them back, perhaps for years. No matter what projections a person places on me, as a chaplain I represent that higher power they might eventually believe in, and they expect more from me than they do from a counselor or nurse.

For instance, the residents know the nurses and counselors label them with diagnoses, and they note what the residents say in their charts. As a chaplain, I do not diagnose, and I can offer an extra layer of confidentiality. Although that confidentiality is not total, because I am a mandated reporter and a member of a team, residents often feel comfortable sharing things with me that they haven't told anyone else.

Occasionally a patient reveals something I need to report to the team, such as when a patient told me she was cutting herself on the unit. Once I felt the need to make a report to child protective services. In such instances, I let the patient know I'm going to pass on what they said, because I do not want them to feel betrayed. I can imagine a situation in which it would be unsafe to let a resident know of my intention to disclose what they told me, and I'm grateful that so far I haven't encountered such a situation. I try to be worthy of the residents' trust.

Staying in the Moment

Of course, no matter what I do or say, I can't fulfill every expectation the residents have of me. Some residents, expecting me to be a "believer," are confused by my refusal to teach them about Christianity or preach during groups. Other residents expect me to give them answers, intervene for them with God, or explain right and wrong.

One man, for instance, wanted to know if I thought he was going to hell because he used heroin. He asked me this in the hallway while I was on my way to a meeting, so I didn't have time to help him process the question, and he wouldn't have wanted to do that, anyway. He wanted a yes or no answer. Surely I, a woman of God, knew the truth about this.

This is dangerous ground. As I've said before, my Unitarian Universalist faith reminds me that I don't know. Personally, I don't believe in heaven, and I sure don't believe in hell, but even if I could have promised this man that no such places exist, and even if I thought it was a good idea to do so, I doubt such an assertion would have helped him. He had already gotten an answer he didn't like from his pastor, yet the answer he hoped for, that he could shoot as much heroin as he wanted and not go to hell, probably would not support his sobriety.

After admitting I didn't know the answer to his question, I sidestepped the talk about heaven and hell by asking about his relationship with God. What was that relationship like when he was loaded? How about when he was straight? What kind of relationship did he think God wanted with him? What kind did he want? Did he want the sober relationship or the drug-affected one?

Therein lay the problem, because he didn't know what he wanted. So I left him to think about it, knowing he might decide to use again. But even if he chose sobriety as the best answer right now, in the morning his decision could change.

Which is true for most addicts. They can't commit to a lifetime of sobriety. That's overwhelming. But, as they say in twelve-step circles, addicts can stay clean and sober one day at a time. Renewing their commitment each day, sometimes each moment, helps people stay clean in the face of anxiety, cravings, and invitations from friends who use drugs. Keeping a focus on the present moment can help.

That's one reason I teach the residents meditation and mindfulness. Mindfulness is the quality of being present and alert to the moment, and meditation teaches us to be mindful.

Meditation can offer a lot of benefits. The practice changes the neurochemical activity in our brain, for instance, increasing our dopamine production. Dopamine is one of the neurotransmitters in our brain that make us feel good, and recent research indicates it helps us pay attention. People who become addicted may not produce enough dopamine to begin with, and then the drugs they use multiply their dopamine receptors so they need more and more dopamine. When they stop using drugs, they feel miserable.

Because meditation increases our production of dopamine, it can speed up a recovering addict's healing process, allowing her to experience joy that much sooner. Meditation also decreases the anxiety, depression, irritability, headaches, and digestive problems that many addicts experience. When they're loaded, they don't have to feel their discomfort. If they meditate, they may find they have less discomfort to avoid.[3]

Because of the emphasis on nonjudgment, meditation can also help us release our shame. How liberating to face the ugly thoughts and shame-based beliefs we have about ourselves and to let the thoughts pass by like clouds, remembering that judgments are stories we have made up.

This practice helps me as a chaplain, as well. When I notice I'm judging a resident, I remember that the judgment isn't reality. The judgment is what I tell myself about reality. My meditation practice encourages me to let go and look, listen, and experience the truth about the person in front of me. If I am able to do this, I can sustain a deep presence that the residents notice.

For instance, one man told me I had "hugged his soul." Years later, he was still sober—not only because he had felt "hugged," of course, but that experience helped him realize he was worthy of recovery. Another time, because I could withhold my judgment, a young woman let go of her self-loathing, looked inside

---

3   While meditation can be a wonderful support in recovery, it is not purely benign. Sitting still for long periods of time can bring up painful memories and anxieties, especially if a person has a history of significant trauma. For that reason, I encourage the residents to work with a teacher, meditate in short bursts, or try walking meditation.

herself, and saw what she imagined God saw in her: a brilliant blue crystal, shimmering with love. The memory of that moment sustained her during some challenging times.

Not everyone who speaks with the chaplain will experience such transformation. Not even those who feel a mystical something stir inside them are guaranteed sobriety. One twenty-year-old described a moving moment when he felt the peace and power of God's presence and knew he was blessed and loved. This inspired him to try, once again, to get clean. Yet as he spent days on the unit, and talked with using friends on the outside, the memory of that presence faded. He left treatment early and relapsed.

This is part of the tragedy of addiction. There are no guarantees, and the disease can take lives. Addicts die of cirrhosis, they get shot, they kill someone while driving. Sometimes they take so many drugs they lose their minds, or they get caught committing a crime and end up in jail.

At other times, though, their recovery lasts.

As long as someone is alive, there is hope. That's why I search for an opening with even the most hardened individual. I plant seeds. Nurturing and tending them is up to the addict.

Empathy, Humility, and Love

In this way, addicts aren't so different from the rest of us. We all have wounds, resentments, shattered dreams. We may do a worse or better job of letting go of our pain, and we may find help on our journey, but ultimately, whether we become free is up to us. In the group I lead on loss, for instance, I point out that addicts aren't the only ones who try to escape feelings of grief. Few people in our country know how to mourn in a healthy manner. We might not use drugs to numb ourselves, but we find other ways to avoid feeling pain. We work too much, exercise too much, stuff ourselves with food, wear ourselves out volunteering. If we do this over a long period of time, these behaviors may look like addictions.

These activities are not bad, nor is it harmful to take a break from grieving. When we've experienced a tragic loss, our minds and bodies go into shock, for a good reason: We can only cope with so much pain at a time. Gerald May notes in *Addiction and Grace* that the destructive effects of our addictions lie less in the ability of our drug or behavior of choice to numb our feelings or bring us relief than "in our *slavery* to these things, turning desire into compulsion, with ugly and loveless consequences for ourselves and our world." What we turn to for comfort can end up controlling our brains and not letting us go.

For instance, I like to keep busy. I also want to be seen as responsible, capable, and reliable. If I believe something needs to be done, and no one else is willing to do it, I feel an urge to jump in and take care of it. You might say I am co-dependent, and I have found twelve-step programs helpful.

Mostly, though, if I exercise regularly, work in the garden, meditate, see my spiritual director, visit with friends and colleagues now and then, and stay connected to my god, I do fine. When I stop taking care of myself, I lose the connections that keep me healthy. Then I relapse on busyness, and I feel stressed, angry, and resentful, and I get sick. So you could call this behavior of mine an addiction.

Perhaps my addiction is not as serious as an addiction to heroin or methamphetamine or gambling. And yet, when I get overwhelmed, I hurt others and I hurt myself. And like the drug or gambling addict, if I want to stay healthy, I will have to manage this addictive tendency of mine for the rest of my life.

When I work with addicts, though, I find it doesn't really matter if I'm an addict myself. As a Unitarian Universalist minister, I respect each person; I feel compassion for and love every soul. Because I'm humble enough to realize that I don't know what God is, that I am still searching for the ultimate purpose of life, and that I have done things I wish I hadn't, I can be nonjudgmental. I also believe that, if it weren't for a genetic fluke and the gift of a loving family, I could be sitting in the semicircle of residents rather than standing at the front of the class.

My first CPE supervisor taught that emotions are sacred, and my Unitarian Universalist values teach that all life has some glimmer of worthiness, so I believe if I am present to the residents, and if I reflect the love of the universe to the best of my ability, we stand in sacred space and do sacred work, and we don't have to have experienced a major addiction to do it. We've all been lonely, scared, empty, angry at God, broken. Everyone experiences loss, shame, resentment. Perhaps we struggle with forgiveness because we have been betrayed and abandoned or because we have betrayed ourselves and others. We may have struggled to find a spiritual path that works for us and a higher power we can believe in. Certainly we have all needed love, and if we have learned to love ourselves, and learned to love someone else, we can offer the addict, or anyone, the most essential healing: We can offer a love that frees, a love that accepts, a love that tells her she deserves happiness, a love that reminds him he was born for more than this addiction.

The Thin Blue Line

LISA PRESLEY

Police chaplaincy is not for the faint of heart. Nor is it for those who leap to judgment, who cannot live in the presence of ambiguity, and who cannot find it in themselves to respect the nearly impossible job that those in law enforcement are asked to undertake. This mostly volunteer work brings incredible challenges and amazing satisfaction to the person willing to venture into it with open mind and heart, and invest the years it will take to be seen as a reliable and useful presence.

Police chaplaincy comes in two different flavors. One is actually chaplaincy to the public, both to victims of crimes and to bystanders. These chaplains may ride with the police, but the focus of their work is the community. The other is chaplaincy to the department, both to officers and to civilian staff (dispatchers, administrative aides, etc.), to help them carry out their work responsibilities and to be there for them and their families in the midst of whatever life throws at them. My chaplaincy experience was primarily the latter; my colleagues and I were there first and foremost for our officers and civilian employees. But through working with them, we also ministered to the civilian population, always at the request of the department.

One of the first things to know about law enforcement agencies is that the Thin Blue Line is alive, well, and much harder to cross than you may imagine. Many law enforcement officers see the world as clearly divided into "us" and "them"—with "them" being a large group that includes the bad guys, those who support and abet them, and those who uncritically challenge the workings of, and even the need for, law enforcement. To be able to cross that gulf takes years—it usually takes a new police chaplaincy program about five years to become fully established and respected within the department. Law enforcement officers need to know that you are truly there with and for them, that you are faithful to your promises to them. They work in the shadow world, at the intersection of poverty, crime, and the failed war on drugs, and they engage with people whose living conditions leave them no hope of escaping that world. Their lives are on the line every day, and they need to know that you will not undermine them or endanger them more.

As a privileged, (over)educated white woman, I lived for years with the luxury of not having to think about or deal with law enforcement agents. My world was safe because of their existence—I did not have to worry much about my physical safety, and I could believe that the police officer was my friend. I know that this is not a universal experience—many people see the police as a threat to their well-being, and there is certainly much that can be criticized about the way policing is carried out. The lives of people of color that have been lost in encounters with law enforcement cannot be discounted, and their number is unacceptably high.

The recent increase in high-profile deaths of African Americans at the hands of the police is alarming. As a former police chaplain, this disturbing trend saddens my heart and spirit deeply. I also believe that we do our law enforcement officers a deep disservice and put them in an impossible position. We ask them to keep people safe without providing them with adequate training and resources. Our officers reflect the prejudice that is embedded in our society and we do not provide them with appropriate ways to critique and understand racism and poverty which would help them effectively de-escalate volatile situations. In addition, the prevalence of weapons in our communities means that every encounter between police and civilians is potentially deadly. Effective gun control and licensing would also reduce officers' fear of being shot, and thereby decrease

their violent responses to threats. Contemporary police chaplains need to understand this complex context, and be willing
to dance between the edges of it—standing up for the ending
of systemic oppression and racism, while also supporting law
enforcement personnel.

At the same time, it is naive to ignore or downplay the fact
that any encounter that the police have with the public could
result in an officer's injury or death. According to the Officer
Down Memorial Page (www.odmp.org), an average of 163 officers died in the line of duty each year between 2001 and 2015.
For the period 2005–2014, more than one-third of line-of-duty
deaths were caused by police officers being shot; another third
were killed in traffic accidents. Each traffic stop or response to
a domestic violence incident or call to a robbery brings the possibility that the officer will not return home that day.

So police chaplaincy occurs where a group of people charged
with bringing safety and security to a world that is significantly
divided by class and race meet people whose lives are made
harder and harsher by laws and policies that disproportionately
impact the disadvantaged. Nearly 30 percent of the suspects
described to police are African American, a proportion that can
be blamed on racial bias in the public at large, not law enforcement. And how many white, non-poor people commit the same
acts for which black people are reported to the police and have
their behavior dismissed with comments such as, "Oh, boys will
be boys"? Both law enforcement officers and people living in
poverty are captives of a system that they did not create, but in
which they live, often to the detriment of them all. Both sides
receive soul injury, and the discerning police chaplain will need
to understand these dilemmas and conundrums in order to help
police officers navigate this intersection.

I began my work with the police in the mid-1990s, in a suburb
of Detroit adjoining the city. I grew up a child of the Sixties, and
in my wildest imagination, I never would have thought about rid-
ing in the front seat of a police car. My family had a long history
of involvement in demonstrations and civil disobedience, and in
most of those settings the police had been seen as part of the
enemy. So when the police chief sent me an invitation to join him

for breakfast to talk about police chaplaincy, I went both out of
curiosity and at the insistence of the congregation's administra-
tor. She had been robbed on the job shortly before I arrived, and
the professional and caring response of the local police led her to
insist I attend the meeting. From the first description of the work,
I was hooked, and I would never have imagined how deeply I
would come to love "my officers," nor how much I would miss
the camaraderie and interaction with them when my life circumstances required me to step away from this work.

My responsibilities as a volunteer police chaplain were simple: attend one meeting a month, ride along with a police officer
for one shift a month, and share on-call rotation. Yet this doesn't
explain the job well, nor the process of being accepted as a valued chaplain.

A ride-along could mean accompanying the officer into a
wide variety of situations—traffic stops, young people shoplift-
ing, car crashes, domestic violence incidents, deaths at home,
people with mental health issues, fires, or an unlocked business that needed to be guarded until the owner could arrive and
secure the premises. It could be eight to ten hours of driving
around with little activity; it could be one thing after another.
The officer and I might be engaged in deep conversation for
hours, or barely say a hundred words to each other, with the
silence being either comfortable or uncomfortable. We chaplains were guests in the squad cars, and some of the officers
appreciated our presence, while others were not quite sure
about us. But the way that mindless boredom could change to
sheer terror in a matter of seconds was something that never
failed to take me by surprise.

When working with civilians, the chaplains were usually
called upon to deal with things that the police did not want
to touch. We were sometimes referred to as the "death squad,"
as they relied upon us to notify the loved ones of people who
had died. These are the memories that stay with me still—
telling an aging mother that her son had fallen out of his high-
rise window; telling a fourteen-year-old that her mother had
died in a car crash right after dropping her off for school; talking
with a grandmother about her grandson, who had been killed

in a drive-by shooting on their front stoop; reading to a family the note that their teenage daughter had left for them before she took her own life. I remember talking with a seven-year-old about how she didn't want to have to go back to live with her family in the city, because she had just gotten used to not having to sleep on the floor to avoid the gunfire outside. I remember the wild joy of returning to her mother the two-year-old that her ex-husband had kidnapped from her house; I remember the satisfaction the officers and I felt when the suspect was found within ten minutes of leaving with his daughter.

My biggest initial surprise was that 90–95 percent of the officers had entered police work for the same reason I went into ministry: to make the world a better place. The methods and location of our work might differ greatly, but not the intent. In my decade of police chaplaincy, I rarely witnessed officers using the power of their position for anything other than to figure out what was going on and discern the best path forward for all involved. Watching how the officers dealt with sexual assault victims and the family members of those who had committed suicide, I was filled with pride and admiration for their humane response.

At the same time, there was a very clear line between right and wrong, and they judged people according to which side of it they were on. I remember the night when it was reported that a woman had been assaulted and injured in her home. Initially, the officers' empathy was palpable. But when they discovered that she supplied drugs to local schoolchildren, their attitude changed dramatically—she got what she deserved, they felt. I remember hearing them say, "When you lie down with dogs, you have to expect to get fleas." As chaplain, I needed to be aware of when to leave such black-and-white thinking alone and when to challenge it, either by asking questions or by reframing the situation. For the most part, I could offer such a challenge only with the officers who already knew and respected me; others would dismiss it as a naive, knee-jerk liberal reaction, and my relationship with them might be damaged. Sometimes the Thin Blue Line could not bear much stretching before it would break, and then re-form with the chaplain on the other side.

The officers' distrust of chaplains was the natural starting place. Just as people in society at large often do, they wondered why we were there, how human we were, whether we were going to try to mess with their minds. Were we agents of the chief, reporting back to him, or could we be trusted to keep their confidences? Were we bleeding hearts who would side with the suspects more than with the officers? What were we really all about? Although clergy often face such questions, I found that the degree of suspicion and the distance between us was greater than in other settings. I also learned that one misstep could set back the development of a trusting relationship by months. Since officers are lied to many times a day, my officers judged me by my actions. "To what extent do your words match your deeds," they wordlessly asked me, "and can I trust you to have my back, literally as well as figuratively?"

This work was a theological challenge for me, and that challenge was brought most directly to me by one of the officers. Dennis was a student of religion; he had grown up without any religious exposure, and his adult studies had taken him to a deep appreciation of, and deep involvement in, his evangelical Christian congregation. He also held one of the broadest understandings of religion I've ever encountered. His beliefs were not unconsidered, but well-thought-out responses to the world he encountered. I remember having to explain homophobia to him; it hadn't occurred to him because, in his words, "It's the lesbian couples in our family who have the best and longest-lasting relationships." This was not something I expected, considering that he was an evangelical Christian. I found myself saying, "Dennis, get back in the box that I had you in!"

One long night, Dennis and I were driving along, and he posed another one of his tough questions. He told me that he taught his nieces and nephews that there was a love story that was written for them, the Bible, and in that book they would learn how deeply and truly they were loved by God, and that with God's strength, they could have amazing lives. He told them that the power of this love was great enough to help them overcome any obstacles and pitfalls that might come, and that the love of Jesus was there for them no matter what. As I listened to him, I could hear echoes of our Universalist ancestors, and I found myself thrilled. But then he asked me, "What do you have that will help children feel safe at night? What do you have that's more attractive than drugs and easy money? What do you have that's powerful enough to change the lives of the youngest of us?"

I'm still not sure if I have a good answer to Dennis's question. Although as an adult I understand and deeply appreciate the value of our First Principle, the "inherent worth and dignity of every person," and I value my own search for wisdom, I can't imagine those Principles holding the love that the seven-year-old girl needed wrapped around her when the gunfire came through her bedroom wall. Yes, our Universalist heritage emphasizing the love of God for everyone is one answer, but there are times I wonder where in our humanistic tradition, or the secularism of many of our Unitarian Universalist congregations, there are words as deeply comforting to children as "there is a love story that's been written for you." I still wrestle with Dennis's question, and he is partly responsible for me now using the word God in speaking of my own faith journey—not because I see God in anthropomorphic ways, but because it's the biggest word I can imagine. From Dennis, and his loving God, I learned how to embrace the language of the Holy, and my life is deeper because of that.

It was also through my police chaplaincy work that I did the deepest ministry of my life. Let me share three short vignettes illustrating the way this ministry shaped and challenged me.

I worked for years with a police family in which the fifteen-year-old son had murdered his twelve-year-old sister. This work took me to the deep questions: What atonement is necessary, both from a community and internally? How can parents who have devoted their lives to an oath to serve and protect cope with the fact that their own children have become a criminal and a victim of violent crime? What does it mean to be in deep connection with someone who has taken another's life? Supporting the parents and their son took me on a journey that stretched and changed me.

One evening, I reported to a situation where a young man had been killed in a drive-by shooting, most likely drug related.

I entered the family's house and sat down next to the young man's grandmother. She and I spoke for twenty minutes, with her telling me about her grandson, and her dreams for him, and her intense grief at his death. We shared sadness and regret, and shed tears. And all of this was done with his grandmother speaking Chaldean and not knowing English, and me speaking English and not knowing Chaldean. Language need not be a barrier in love and loss.

On another evening, I accompanied officers when they responded to the suicide of a teenager in her family's home. Walking in, I met the parents and siblings, all huddled together, not saying much, in the living room. I sat with them for a while, asking stories about their daughter and sister. I then asked if I could go see her, and they thanked me for doing so. In her bedroom, the officers and I talked about the tragedy of this kind of loss as they completed their investigation. When the medical examiner came to collect her body, I worked with the officers to move the family to another part of the house, where they would not have to see, and then suggested to them that I stay with her until her body was removed. They agreed, and I stood as a witness of hope and love during that process. I learned from the sergeant on site that she had written letters to her family, and I asked if I could read the letters to them before they were taken away as evidence. The sergeant agreed, and I did so. Then, returning the letters to the sergeant, I made an offhand remark about these being the last treasures they would receive from this young woman. The sergeant left, and I stayed with the family as the other officers completed their work. About twenty minutes later, the sergeant was back. Having considered my comment about the letters being treasures, he had decided to photocopy them and enter the copies into evidence, so that the family could keep the originals. The sergeant said that without my presence, he wouldn't have thought to do that, but that my ministry with the family helped him see the suicide in a different light. He thanked me, as I thanked him on their behalf.

Each one of these situations reminded me of the power of the Holy in the presence of unexpected loss and intense grief. Because of my clerical collar, they were willing to give over to me the power and honor of being the presence of the Holy, of God, in ways that too rarely happen in parish-based ministry. I could, in some ways, slip into the anonymity of the role and thereby serve the families better, whereas in parish ministry my own being, and my congregants' history of relationships with me, can get in the way. In police chaplaincy the roles were clear and temporary, and thus allowed for a deeper sense of connection. Liminality provides that safe space, for a time. People were sometimes more able to express themselves authentically because they knew they would not be judged later for whatever humanness they showed now, in the present. I learned to be humble at these times, knowing that what was happening truly wasn't about me, and I learned to recognize the privilege of standing alongside people, bringing the face of the Holy to the hardest times in their lives. At the same time, police chaplaincy helped open me to the limits of my assumptions, to the need to deepen my spiritual connections and to understand that life is rarely either/or but more often both/and. The questions I had to deal with—who are the "good guys" and "bad guys" in any situation, what does salvation mean, how do I listen and speak in the face of "evil," how do I even know what evil is—all of these deepened my sense of self and of calling.

Police chaplaincy is not for the faint of heart. It is not for those who want the world to make sense, for there to be good guys and bad guys with a clear line delineating them. It is hard to maintain the Unitarian Universalist call for social justice while working with those whom many in our congregations would condemn for their vocational choice. It is, by and large, a volunteer ministry. It is also a ministry where one must be at home with one's self and with what people project onto those they see as representatives of God. Wearing a clerical collar meant that my ministry was not about me—rather, I represented the Holy, for good or ill. Telling people of their loved one's demise; being present as grief became real; watching as people were arrested for heinous crimes; being shunned both by those within the department who have no use for chaplains, and by those within Unitarian Universalism who have no use for anyone in law enforcement; being challenged by ministerial colleagues who thought (and said) I was "consorting with the enemy"; standing on the side of love with a "Black Lives Matter" button on, while believing in the humanity of those on the other side of the Thin Blue Line. All of this—yes, all of this—is the ministry of my heart. It is an amazing ministry, if you can live in the ambiguity of injustice and imperfect humanity. It is a ministry that will stretch your heart in ways my parish ministry never has, and let you know that who you are makes a real difference.

Beloved Community
Across Prison Walls

MANDY GOHEEN

The Church of the Larger Fellowship (CLF) is a global congregation that connects Unitarian Universalists—wherever in
the world their spiritual journeys have taken them. All kinds of
people from across the globe make up this congregation of more
than 3,500 members, the majority of whom interact primarily
through social media and attend live-stream worship services.
The online resources available through the CLF are extensive
and ever expanding. But more than 730 of our members do not
have access to our community in this way—these members live
in prisons and jails across the United States.

In the late 1960s the CLF welcomed its first incarcerated
member. When I started as a learning fellow at the CLF in 2014,
about 550 of our members joined us from prison. As of May
2016, our congregation has 730 prison members, with more
joining every week. Amazingly, the CLF has never recruited
people from prison. Our growth has all been word-of-mouth
evangelism, beginning with that first member in the 1960s. Our
literature has passed from hand to hand, along with the good
news that Unitarian Universalism and the CLF believe that all
people are inherently worthy and are welcome as members of
our congregation. Once they join they are given the opportunity
to grow spiritually and build relationships with other Unitarian

Universalists. Spiritual maturity and relationships are critical components to building hope and saving lives.

In the over ten years past that I have been a member of the CLF, you all have been a constant and enriching source of strength and encouragement to my self. As a transgender prisoner serving a life without parole, I need all of the spiritual help and encouragement I can get. I am also a Wiccan which is my Third Strike of Social Unacceptability. But apparently not for the CLF. I have been welcomed and accepted. You have truly enriched my life.

—Donna, CLF member in prison

With our home office located at the UUA headquarters in Boston, the CLF Prison Ministry has acted on behalf of Unitarian Universalism to serve the incarcerated. Originally, the CLF was hesitant to step into the work of our 2005 Statement of Conscience addressing Criminal Justice and Prisoner Reform. Our leaders were concerned that our members in prison would be denied our programming if we became politically engaged. However, given the current escalating culture of police brutality, the CLF decided to support the Black Lives Matter Movement very seriously—well before the 2015 Action of Immediate Witness calling on Unitarian Universalists to do so.

As times change and our numbers grow we have adopted a more creative approach to the way we do the work of prison ministry to such a decentralized group of people. We are developing networks and partnerships so that we can be fully committed to supporting our members in prison and work toward the end of mass incarceration.

Waking Up

What are you waiting for? I have decided not to wait. I will not wait for the future to saunter up and greet me. I will not wait for my hopes, dreams, and prayers to fall into my lap. I will rise up each morning and praise the glory of the day. I shall stride forward with my head held high and with Love in

my heart. I shall give up my doubts and fears unto the hands
of God with every breath and step I take. I will live and make
the world a better place.

—Mark, CLF member in prison

In 2013 if you had told me I would be starting seminary the
next year and I would be the Church of the Larger Fellowship's
Director of Prison Ministry, I would have asked you what planet
you were from. Others might have seen it coming but I was
oblivious to my path. I had felt the calling to work with people during my time as a foster parent, but ministry was never
something I had seriously considered and prison ministry was
nowhere on my radar. But as with so many calling stories, a
small voice changed everything.

One early spring day I was driving my kids to school, and
men in black and white stripes were weed-eating under the oaks
in the cemetery across the street from the Montgomery city jail.
The small voice spoke from the back seat and said, "Mommy, I
have a question." Isaiah always has a question. In that impatient
voice that parents use after the millionth question of the morning, I said, with a sigh, "What's your question?"

"I was wondering," which is how he starts every question,
"why are all the boys in jail brown boys like me?"

The world tipped sideways. I choked on my words, "Isaiah,
I don't know, but I promise I will do whatever I can to figure it
out." That was the minute I woke up and realized how white I
was, how much I didn't know, and that if this precious child was
to survive I had to do something. Desperate for answers, I asked
a professor of ethics from Tuskegee University, who was visiting
my Unitarian Universalist congregation the very next Sunday. I
told her what had happened and asked her what I should have
said. Her answer was as jarring as the original question: "You
should have told him the truth."

Stepping Foot into a Prison

On a path to answer my son's question, I began a fellowship position with the CLF's prison ministry in my second semester of

seminary. In all honesty, other than an undergraduate field trip, I had never set foot in a prison before I began my work at the CLF. Within a month, I was inside a prison, alone, with a room full of women, leading a meditation and stress-management class. The prison chaplain at the CLF at the time was Rev. Patty Franz. She told me that I was either going to love teaching or not be able to do it; there was no in-between. It was hard. It was humbling. And by my third class, I was absolutely in love with it.

I still had a lot to learn, but loving the work helps. The women needed someone to listen and stay present, no matter how hard it was to hear the truths they needed to tell. A couple of weeks into the class, I began thinking about the seven women who regularly attended the group, trying to hold them in my heart with loving-kindness. Thanksgiving was the following week and I couldn't stop thinking about what it must be like to be in prison during the holidays. I let my worry distract me with the "what if" scenarios.

What if I was in prison on Thanksgiving? I don't even like holidays and Thanksgiving is my least favorite. But prison? I stewed about how awful it was going to be for them and how I needed to do something to protect these women from being sad on Thanksgiving. By the time we met, I had a plan. Our class began with a guided meditation, followed by a mindfulness lesson and check-in. Me—the big-stuff, privileged, free-world, pseudo-Buddhist wannabe, meditation teacher—solemnly, and with great sensitivity and political correctness, opened the check-in by saying, "I just can't imagine how hard it is going to be spending Thanksgiving here in prison. Let's check in about how you're feeling about it and see if we can come up with some mindfulness strategies to help you get through the holiday away from your family."

An awkward silence ensued. One of the women put her elbows on her knees and rested her chin on her fists, making strong eye contact with me. "You don't get it. If I wasn't here I would be out there getting high, not with my family. Out there Thanksgiving is just another day, nothing special. In here I am sober and I get to eat." This was the first test of many over the next hour to see if I could be trusted. I sat there smiling and listening. Each time I wanted to run away, I thought about the advice my grandmother had given me when parenting got tough: "Just love them."

The CLF Letter Writing Ministry

At the CLF Prison Ministry, we refer to the non-incarcerated side of the partnership as our "free-world pen pals" or members of the Letter Writing Ministry Team. In my first few months I reached out to this team—exchanging emails and talking on the phone with more than eighty Unitarian Universalists. In the midst of my conversations, I began to recognize some patterns. In the "good" matches between a free-world pen pal and an incarcerated member, both sides were open and/or able to create deep connections and the ministry flowed in both directions. It was crucial that both members benefitted spiritually. The best partners also respected each other's privacy and path of spiritual growth. Unfortunately, the second thing I observed is that ultimately not all matches work. Being a free-world pen pal is not easy work, and having good boundaries is essential to success. In these situations, then as now, the CLF staff and members talked through what did work with the match, tried to resolve any boundary issues, and determined whether it was time to quit.

There are many amazing stories and moments that we are proud to have fostered at the CLF's prison ministry. One of my favorites is summed up in the following email:

Mrs. Goheen,
Greetings, my name is James Ortiz. I have been a prisoner member with the CLF for ~ 8 years. I went through the ministry when Rev. Pat was running it, and I went through the New UU course. While I was taking other classes, I received an invite asking if I wanted a Pen Pal, I said yes and I got the agreement in the mail, signed it, and was matched. I still write to Vickie, and I am very good friends with Lynn. The letter-writing ministry brought me

closer to UUs and afforded me the fellowship I could not find in prison.

I was released March 28th. My brother, Mario, and Lynn (yes, my CLF Pen Pal) were there to pick me up and drive me home to Texas. It was a wonderful experience and their presence helped me enter the world again in the hands of two people I knew that love me and care for me.

I found steady employment in 3 days as an electrician's mechanic. It don't pay much (I would make more money working at McDonald's) but I am learning a lot and the job provides me with a view of how things are done in the construction trade. I will be starting my own business in the next 12 months.

I have found a local UU church I have been attending. They are wonderful and Rev. Kathy knows all about my background through Lynn. Before I was even released, we knew I wanted to go to a brick and mortar church to meet people, good people of like mind and who have the 7 principles in heart. After all, that is what brings us all together, isn't it. J. Lynn found 1 UU close to my future residence. Rev. Kathy and everyone I have met so far are great!

I have had such a good experience with the letter-writing ministry that I want to give back by taking on a prisoner to write to. I have dedicated my Sundays as my Divine time. My church gathers on Sundays, and has many other programs scattered through the week. But I reserve Sundays for church and church activities. One thing I wish to do is dedicate the time to write a prisoner member. Then I noticed this on the website:

> You must affirm you have not been arrested, incarcerated, or on parole or probation in the prior 12 months.

Is that set in stone or just paper? Because I just got released in March, do I have to wait until my one-year anniversary in order to fulfill this promise of mine? Maybe I don't understand the reasoning behind this requirement, but although I am constantly growing and improving myself, basically I am going to be the same person with the same morals and values a year from now as I am today. Well, hopefully my life will improve some as I work on my future. But what is the difference if I write now or a year from now? I have been a UU for almost a decade now. I have extensive experience in the letter-writing ministry and I come with good references.

Have a Great Day
James

I responded almost immediately to James's email, clarifying that the requirement to not have been incarcerated for at least a year applied to people that the CLF was unfamiliar with. Of course he could be a pen pal! I don't know if I was more excited about James using the CLF to launch himself into a brick-and-mortar Unitarian Universalist congregation or that he questioned the rules of the CLF. James is now a free-world pen pal and we email regularly. His story fills me with joy.

However, not every match is "beer and skittles," as one member of our letter-writing team would put it. Her story is also a CLF success story, but in a different way. She has worked through difficult situations and has repeatedly had to set boundaries with her pen pal. No matter how many outs I give her, she continues to write—her commitment to the inherent worth of her pen pal is inspirational. Here is her story in her own words, edited for length:

> Dwayne and I were matched as pen pals through the CLF prison ministry. CLF's only expectations from participants is an exchange of friendly letters on topics of mutual interest—that didn't sound too hard. We introduced ourselves and I discovered that my pen pal, Dwayne, was a young, straight, white male. He wrote in his introduction that "I like to smile and enjoy life and make others smile and feel good about themselves. I like to listen. If you're

having any problems, I like to help people." I began by discussing my spirituality, "Before I was UU, I was Catholic, then Quaker. My current private spiritual practice incorporates elements of all of the above." Dwayne responded, "I'm eclectic; I'm into astrology, tarot, and I'm studying LDS (Mormonism)."

In his next letter, he asked, "What have you learned about yourself since you were 50?"

I wrote back, "I've learned I'm a lesbian, a writer, and a damn good dog trainer. Since 50, I don't swallow what 'everybody' believes. Also I've learned that I have the kind of body that gains strength easily." I sent my response and waited for his next letter.

At the end of his next letter, however, he asked, "What is your exact date and time of birth? I want to do your chart." I hesitated. I had been sending my letters to him through my office because the last thing I wanted was to have him sitting on my doorstep when he got out. Hence, I was reluctant to give him such identifying information. So I ignored that question, as per CLF guidelines. The guidelines also mention that "some prisoners will honor your boundaries; others will try to see how much they can get from you."

Dwayne decided to push the boundaries. "I can't be intimate with you if I don't know your full name and birth date. Maybe Sharon isn't really your name." Ignoring Dwayne's requests hadn't worked. My response was firm, "I'm not giving out identifying information like my full name, date of birth or Social Security Number. Sharon is the name you will know me by." That ultimatum ended his requests for identifying information.

Then Dwayne began making romantic overtures. "Please don't be offended, but I must say you sound very good looking." I reminded him that CLF letter-writing guidelines forbid romantic pursuits and that our letters must remain platonic. To move things onto a less personal level, I shared some of my writing on the intersection of science and politics. He told me writing was like his secret mistress and he submitted work to prison writing web-

sites. His next letter sent me to a site with a poem graphi-
cally describing everything Dwayne would like to do to
"Sharon, a 75-year-old lesbian."
      Me writhing naked on the Internet! I discussed the
issues with Mandy at CLF. She was supportive, as always:
"I think your letter is caring and respectful and I would
like this to be his last chance to straighten up. He has not
been very easy to correspond with. If he pushes things
with you one more time [CLF] will be the bad guy and
end the match."
      I wrote to Dwayne, "It was NOT OK to identify me.
If you overstep the boundaries again, our correspondence
will stop." Firm boundaries have stopped the sexual
advances and his requests for identifying personal information, although Dwayne asks for favors in almost every
letter. Some I grant; most I don't.
      Although I'd hoped to be paired with someone who
illegally copied DVDs or committed a minor drug offense,
I discovered Dwayne was serving twenty years for child
sexual abuse. I believe even sexual predators have inherent worth and dignity. However, the rest of us need to be
protected from them.

Opening Space for Growth

Many free-world people who request to be pen pals cannot be
matched to our members in prison. Free-world Unitarian Universalists have their hearts in the right place but many of them
can't imagine writing to someone who has been labeled by society as violent. Humanizing someone with the label of prisoner
is the first hurdle a free-world pen pal must overcome. Separating the person from the crime they have been sentenced for is
the work of justice. As in the story above, it is not always easy to
have faith in the inherent worth of someone who doesn't understand relationships. But that is how the CLF Prison Ministry
works—one relationship at a time.
      Thankfully we are not alone. There are countless groups
across the country doing both secular and faith-based work

that hold close the values of our first Principle. We at the CLF envision a future where our prison ministry continues to grow and build in a community of collaborators who are also working to build relationships and end mass incarceration. To this end, we have just launched our new program, the Worthy Now Network. This new initiative invites people on both sides of prison walls into beloved community. It goes deeper than mission work or ministry to the people in prison—our call is to build relationships in an inclusive, justice-seeking community that makes liberal religious values accessible to people who are incarcerated. The Worthy Now Network has three components. It calls on its members to connect with free and incarcerated Unitarian Universalists, deepen their identity as justice-makers and members of the larger CLF community, and act to build relationships and work for justice.

Being part of the CLF these past two years has been an incredible journey and I am blessed to serve a church that gives me the space to dream big. Serving 730 members in 42 different states is a daunting endeavor that requires big dreams. I find hope in this ministry, in which networks of support cross the boundaries constructed by mass incarceration. This hope strengthens my belief that the small voice of my future grandchild will never ask, "Why are all the boys in jail brown boys like me?"

The Training of Chaplains

KAREN L. HUTT

Why become a chaplain? Do chaplains feel an existential call to be with people in crisis? Are these caregivers motivated by the hope and practice of healing? Is there a lively fire in their bellies for social change through caregiving? Are they especially suited to stand alongside others, facing death and distress? Do these ministers, rabbis, and imams, these pagans, Buddhists, and humanists, possess an ability to dive deep into the multifaceted nature of the human condition? Or are they spiritual leaders who have grown weary of congregational service and are seeking a new mode of ministry? Whatever someone's reason for or route to chaplaincy, they must satisfy three basic requirements to be certified by the Board of Chaplaincy Certification and enter into a career as a professional chaplain in the United States. First, they must have a master of divinity degree. Second, they must be endorsed by a faith community. Finally, they must complete four units of Clinical Pastoral Education (CPE). Only then can they be considered for board certification and professional chaplaincy.

What Is CPE?

CPE is a form of adult education involving both action and reflection that is pursued in a clinical setting—that is, through work in health care institutions or other community settings. In most CPE groups, six students from diverse theological and philosophical backgrounds spend twelve weeks studying and working together full-time. They might include Roman Catholics, evangelical Christians, Jews, Buddhists, Muslims, Unitarian Universalists, Mormons, Lutherans, secular humanists, and Baptists. This diversity makes for rich and challenging discussions about how spiritual care is understood and provided. In addition to meeting in small groups for reflection and discussion, CPE students—both lay and ordained—are assigned (under supervision) to people seeking spiritual or pastoral care in hospitals, outpatient clinics, prisons, rehab centers, the military, and universities. They are trained to listen, to make spiritual assessments, and to collaborate on multidisciplinary care and treatment plans whose goal is the welfare and healing of the care seeker. Students must face the challenge of remaining true to their own faith tradition while providing spiritual care to patients with different ones or none.

As part of their education, CPE students typically compose summaries, or "verbatims," of their pastoral care encounters, in which they reflect upon what occurred and draw insight from these reflections that they can use in future pastoral care. The performative, improvisational nature of CPE requires students to constantly assess what they have learned about themselves and others in these encounters. Students must be fully open to increasing their self-awareness and their sociocultural understanding. While classroom teaching and instruction in the use of psychological inventories and assessment tools can provide a framework for spiritual care, the unpredictable process of developing relationships with strangers in crisis, and the ambiguity that students must navigate in doing so, form the foundation of chaplains' training.

Although the practice of pastoral care has a long tradition in Christianity and to some extent in other faith traditions, it began to be systematically analyzed, in the way that is now associated with Clinical Pastoral Education, only in the early twentieth century. In 1925, Richard C. Cabot, a prominent physician and active Unitarian layman in Boston and the father of medical social work, published the article "A Plea for a Clinical Year for Theological Students." The concept was enlarged by Anton T. Boisen to include theological inquiry through case studies, the study of "living human documents." Boisen believed that medical or mental health crises have creative possibilities and can be associated with religious "quickening" and with reflection on life's meaning and purpose. In his *Religion in Crisis and Custom*, he writes, "In times of crisis, when the person's fate is hanging in the balance, we are likely to think and feel intensely regarding the things that matter most."

The first clinical pastoral education program was established at Worcester State Hospital, where Boisen was chaplain, in the summer of 1925. The students served as ward attendants during the day, attended staff meetings, and in the evening participated in seminars with Boisen and members of the professional staff. Each year an increasing number of theological students enrolled in this radical new method of theological learning.

On January 21, 1930, Richard Cabot, Bishop Henry Wise Hobson of the Episcopal Church, Samuel Eliot of the Arlington Street Unitarian Church of Boston, William A. Healy of the Judge Baker Foundation, and Ashley Day Leavitt of the Harvard Congregational Church met in Eliot's study, adopted a constitution and bylaws, and signed the incorporation papers for the Council for Clinical Training of Theological Students. Over the years a series of mergers with other denominations and pastoral counseling organizations have created the current Association of Clinical Pastoral Education (ACPE).

The religious liberals associated with the development of CPE easily bridged the gap between science and religion. Many of them were anchored in the progressive education movement of John Dewey and the development of psychological and behavioral constructs that illuminated the nature of human motivation and behavior. They were trailblazers who combined clinical training and practical theology to create a new model for reflection and caregiving, more rooted in narrative theology than in biblical prescriptives for human suffering.

Becoming a CPE Supervisor

To develop as chaplains, students must use their CPE experiences to explore and integrate their pastoral presence, authority, and competencies. Often this prompts them to consider their personal difficulties, triggers, and challenges that may hinder their development of healthy boundaries or relational professionalism. Their supervisors, therefore, must develop theoretical frameworks that will inform how they teach, lead, and train students preparing for spiritual care ministry.

CPE supervisory training can take up to four years to complete, and during that time candidates must explore their understanding of the divine, suffering, caregiving, personhood, narrative hermeneutics, and educational theory. My own practice as a clinical pastoral educator is informed by theoretical constructs from postmodern critical theory, philosophy, practical theology, progressive education, the open classroom movement, social psychology, medical anthropology, and my tradition as a Unitarian Universalist.

The Art of Supervision

While I do not have a concept of a personal God, I understand that personal relationships with the divine are common in all cultures. Therefore, I try to get to know the foundational stories of the CPE students I supervise—what they believe, who they understand themselves to be, how their life experiences play into their theologies, and how these narratives may impact those they serve as chaplains. As I journey with students, I assess how these base narratives interact with the multifaceted clinical stories they are hearing and constructing with care seekers in the hospital, the prison, or the rehab facility. This helps me to ascertain where we might find the creative space to walk together in spite of our differing theological stances. While my theological understanding of God as creativity might not be helpful or even acceptable to my students for their own use, it provides me with the open-mindedness and responsiveness to enter into authentic relationship with them across what can seem like a chasm of difference. I understand that my students are defined and shaped by their past experiences, present choices, future goals, and relational contexts, including their relationship with any ultimate religious reality they may have chosen for themselves. Yet in the course of CPE, their long-held religious beliefs and current social locations are often challenged, as theological constructs and clinical experiences mingle to create new meanings and conflicts.

For example, my CPE student Jerry, a middle-class Missionary Baptist pastor, meets a poor patient who has just had an abortion. He has to negotiate the tension and ambiguity between a tradition that abhors abortion and a duty to care for the person he meets. He also feels particular compassion because she is his daughter's age. In the clinical and group experiences, these tensions can encourage students to broaden their communities of mutual understanding and support. My goal in supervision is to create space for that theological creativity, where clinical and group experiences become the "playground" for experimentation, risk-taking, and adventure. My challenge as a CPE supervisor is to help create a playground that is generous enough for scriptural see-saws, theological swings, and slides toward multiple ultimate realities. Throughout this adventure, students should feel that their belief systems are being both affirmed and stimulated, and that they are becoming better able to reflect, change, and adapt as needed.

As students create relationships with patients, their peers, and their supervisor, and as they watch patients adapt to life-altering conditions, I want them to explore the dynamism of change. My clinical goal is that students pay attention to the incongruent processes that pick at the web of the theological lives that have shaped them, so they can connect and understand the similar processes at work in the lives of the patients they serve.

CPE is a process that intentionally challenges preconceived ways of thinking that do not always lead students on linear paths. A student may have an ideal of silent suffering, but if they are hurt by a supervisor's challenge to their clinical work and say, "Ouch, that hurts!" the ideal may be disrupted. As a result, that student might explore a range of pain thresholds and discover new understandings of suffering in listening to the stories of those they serve. Christian CPE students, for instance, may base much of their orientation to life on the premodern and modern symbols of their faith, and they should be guided not to give them up, but rather to put them in relationship with authentic understandings of their clinical experiences. I want all students to learn to identify, articulate, and affirm their theological experiences and traditions, while doing the work of pastoral care with those who express different spiritualities.

For example, Mira, a devout lay Catholic woman, discovered during her CPE training that she was wedded to the liturgy of the Church, but not to its doctrine regarding the role of women. The first time she ever expressed this was with women clergy from Protestant denominations in her CPE group. As her supervisor, I encouraged her, when it was her turn to lead the group's worship, to create a liturgy in which women had a prominent role. Here, my theology encouraged imagination and creativity within the context of her faith tradition, and designing the worship service helped her to consider what path she might take in the church's future. In their group experience, I encourage students to connect seemingly unrelated experiences and relationships to create new frameworks for theological premises. My theology and supervisory practice compel me to set aside preconceptions, critical judgment, and experiential caution to create theological relationships with students who are filled with imagination and creativity. I seek to help them find value and relevance through the distillation of many theological and philosophical points of view. This task is spiritually enriched by the courage to say "yes" to the unfamiliar, the new, the created.

Gene is very clear about his identity as a Christian. He comes from a family of ministers in the Baptist tradition, has led mission work in Rwanda and Bible studies with homeless men in an urban shelter, and lives in an apartment building of young adult Christians. In CPE his Christian voice was clear and firm, filled with determination and doctrine. Yet another, less-certain ethical voice that was prophetic and oppositional to the church was also emerging. He brought both voices to his clinical work, wanting patients to pray more and rely on God, while also yearning to confront the injustices associated with the poverty that caused them to suffer. My Unitarian Universalist Principles and Purposes influenced my assessment and guided my interventions with him. I believe that authority comes not just from creeds and religious tradition, but also from each person's "direct experience of that transcending mystery and wonder, affirmed in all cultures, which moves us to a renewal of the spirit and an openness to the forces which create and uphold life." Thus, I encouraged Gene to let both voices live in communion as he created a generative relationship between them. I observed his increasing ability to do this when a pagan patient offered to do a prophetic reading of his life. Gene told me that before beginning CPE, he probably would not have talked to people who were not Christians. "I know what scripture says about sorcery and card reading," he said, "but still I recognized this as an experience I would have never had except here in the diversity of this hospital." Although the voice of his tradition still spoke to him, he was able to also listen to his own inner voice, which enabled him to be present to the creative spirit present in this interaction. As Gene realized that how someone receives pastoral care is inextricable from their social location, ethnicity, class, age, and culture, he went deeper with this pagan patient and was able to be in creative communion with her as she shared the traumatizing abuse she had experienced, which was ultimately central to her narrative connection with him. Gene noted that it was in ambiguity and mystery that he was able to "find some connection for me to care for her."

Although the student is the primary agent of change, the supervisor brings respectful curiosity, clinical expertise, and a vested interest in the process. The students and I recognize that they will sometimes be upset or distressed by this collaborative process, and will sometimes resist it. But we all understand that these feelings are necessary components of significant human change and emotional awareness. I want students to explore their possibilities, strengths, personal resources, and resilience as they seek the promises inherent in lifelong change. In dialogue with students, I am primarily concerned with assessing the viability, not the validity, of their personal creations, choices, and behaviors.

Malcolm is a male pastor who leads a suburban Lutheran church—his first such position—and is doing his first unit of

CPE. He tells me that he is concerned about his lack of assertiveness. He has been aware of this aspect of himself for years, but is beginning to see how it hinders his relationships in the student group and with patients and families. In my practice with him, I am inspired to recognize him as the architect of his own reality, and I ask him to describe the construct of non-assertiveness and its function in his life. Then we explore his feelings about, and images and metaphors for, non-assertiveness. He begins to claim that his lack of assertiveness sometimes serves him well as a chaplain, because he is very patient and listens well. I ask him to explore when his non-assertiveness has been a significant problem and when it has not, and to rank his lack of assertiveness on a scale. "Using the metaphors, feelings, and symbols you selected to describe this lack of assertiveness," I say, "tell me what is stopping you from moving in the direction you seek on this scale." He identifies feelings of fear and uncertainty. I then ask him to place his fear and uncertainty on the scale and to explore what it would take to move just one point in the direction he wishes to go. He describes a series of minute changes in his tone, posture, and handshake that would indicate to him that he has moved on the scale. He is starting to envision, and thus embody, a more powerful and assertive self. He goes on to construct and plan a series of responses to situations that have required "a more assertive Malcolm to show up." We explore these responses and look at the strengths and resilience, as well as the fear and resistance, that he is bringing to each situation. In particular, he says that using a firmer handshake at the beginning of an interaction reminds him that he is more powerful and capable than he usually feels. Making the link between self-concept, motivation, and action-learning will serve him well in chaplaincy.

A Unitarian Universalist Theology of CPE Supervision

My humanistic orientation to supervision and education is well matched to the empiricism of Boisen, the founder of CPE, who created models, metaphors, and symbols that express humankind's best understanding of life on the basis of real elements of the human condition rather than theological formulas. Boisen writes, "Religious experience is rooted in the social nature of man and arises spontaneously under the pressure of a crisis situation. We frequently find the sense of contact with the ultimate reality to which we give the name of God. This means a new awareness of the individual's continuity with society at its best." This understanding firmly grounds my supervisory practice in the tradition of social communitarians that is evident in the Principles and Purposes of my Unitarian Universalist faith. I strive to widen my cultural and religious horizons as a Unitarian Universalist clinical supervisor. I am committed to developing and exhibiting cultural humility, which impels me to have direct, authentic experiences with many traditions and faith communities beyond the confines of the CPE seminar. Unitarian Universalism is immensely compatible with the goals and outcomes of Clinical Pastoral Education because our faith is extremely inclusive, with room for the theist, the atheist, the Buddhist, and the religious humanist. As a Unitarian Universalist supervisor, I commit to remaining willing to have a change of heart, maintaining an ethos of care and compassion, and cultivating an ethic of acceptance. My theology holds that there are multiple approaches to life's biggest questions, therefore I believe CPE supervision should validate, provoke, and inspire purposeful and meaningful dialogue across barriers of theology and tradition. Above all, a Unitarian Universalist CPE supervisory theology should be useful, helping student chaplains realize their human potential to the greatest extent possible. For those in crisis, it should facilitate valued and cherished relationships where the spirit of human agency allows meaning and hope to be continually reborn.

Moving Forward
and Looking Back

KAREN L. HUTT

In 1990 Rev. Barbara Kulcher delivered an address to the St. Lawrence Unitarian Universalist District that described the trajectory of Unitarian Universalists in pastoral care. She noted that, historically, Unitarian Universalist ministers have been known more for leadership in social reform movements than for theological leadership in the practice of pastoral care. Much of her talk centered on the work of Rev. Carl Wennestrom, who was the dean of students at Meadville Lombard in the early 1950s and in 1956 became the first chaplain at the University of Chicago Clinics. Wennestrom was interested in the "liberal paradox" of a purposeful commitment to rationality combined with insufficient attention to human suffering and the challenges of being human. "Even in what is very best about us," he wrote,

> We liberals too have sinned and fallen short; or more aptly, perhaps, have fallen out of the wrong side of the bed. Our rationalism has been used not just to defend reason and science and learning and inquiry, but also to defend us from feeling and involvement and emotion and concreteness . . . . Our sense of optimal distance happily prevents us from equating acquiescence or resignation with justice

or fulfillment. It sends us on ahead to prepare the way, to prevent, to educate, to get at root causes, to mobilize public opinion, to serve, if need be, as the community's conscience. Yet our acknowledged anxiety too often keeps us away from the places where concrete suffering is being faced or endured or encountered.

In 1963 Wennestrom died, leaving behind an unfinished doctoral thesis in which he explored this paradox as both a theologian and a clinician. In 1970 John Luther Adams and Seward Hiltner published his unfinished work, together with that of other contributors, in an edited volume titled *Pastoral Care in the Liberal Church*. This volume highlighted the tensions between head and heart that were endemic in many mid-century Unitarian Universalist churches. The classical modernist liberal UU orientation, which makes us reliant on human ability, intellectual stamina, and cognitive powers, left little room for the moving of the spirit, human frailty, distress, and psychosocial dysregulation. While religious liberals were among the first to embrace the scientific discoveries that revealed the complex intricacies of human nature, they were less likely to incorporate these learnings into the care of congregants. Many Unitarian Universalist ministers and congregations understood *care* as advocacy for the amelioration of social ills, the promotion of mental health, and charitable efforts to collect food and clothing for the poor. This outward gaze, seeing *service* as directed to others rather than meaning the care of souls in their congregations, has influenced Unitarian Universalism at several points in our history. In the early 1970s, when Adams and Hiltner's volume was released, Unitarian Universalist churches and fellowships were nearly consumed by the social and political upheaval that had started in the Sixties with the civil rights and anti-war movements. I remember a friend saying that during that time they would go to the Unitarian Universalist church to get their social justice and political information, and to the Lutheran church to get pastoral care. Many UU churches, particularly in the Western Conference, did not seek to arouse emotions and meet emotional needs as much as most other houses of worship around the world did.

Trends and Changes in Pastoral Care in Congregations

Over the past thirty years, a number of trends have made pastoral and spiritual care a greater focus in our churches. First, ministers are required to do Clinical Pastoral Education (CPE), and more and more ministerial students are doing year-long CPE residencies as part of their discernment process. In addition, there are more spiritual care courses in the core seminary curriculum. Second, many more seminarians are coming to ministry from previous careers in psychosocial professions (such as social work, therapy, and psychology), bringing with them foundational caring skills that they often integrate into their call to ministry. Finally, many younger Unitarian Universalist ministers are not wedded to the strictly nontheistic and spiritless language and liturgy that have dominated our worship services. Many have incorporated into worship what they learned in CPE and have encouraged congregations to develop more holistic, spirit-filled modalities that include caring teams, support groups, and covenanting groups. An online search for UU pastoral care teams will yield hundreds of hits: descriptions of such teams, manuals of how to offer such care, and stories of providing it to their congregations. The people who undertake these ministries are trained to know how to listen, recognize people's needs, be sensitive and empathetic, guide or prompt spiritual thinking, and support the search for spiritual practices. Like chaplains in the hospital or hospice, they can be recorders of life events, attitudes, attributes, desires for how a life should end, and other recollections and yearnings. Throughout the country, these UU caregivers serve as nonjudgmental listeners and discussion partners, offering people seeking care a companion with whom to thoughtfully explore hope, meaning, and purpose in their lives.

Trends and Changes in Pastoral Care in Institutional Chaplaincy

In 1991, the year after Kulcher delivered her address, the General Assembly of the UUA wrote community ministry into its bylaws, and the Ministerial Fellowship Committee began granting fellowship to community ministers. Community ministry was now recognized as a legitimate option for ministry outside of the parish. Unitarian Universalist ministers could become chaplains in secular institutions and still retain their status as UU ministers in full fellowship. The change was motivated both by a sense of fairness to ministers already working in community settings and by a vision of increased social outreach through ministry. In a 1995 paper titled "Defining Community Ministry" Dan Hotchkiss, the ministerial settlement director for the UUA, stated,

> Behind the UUA's recognition of community ministry lies the conviction that the UU movement has a mission and an opportunity beyond our congregations. To succeed in this larger sphere we need ministers with special training and a special calling to ministry outside the parish. This is not a new idea for Unitarian Universalists, but neither is it a field where we have distinguished ourselves. A few other denominations have a strong ministerial presence in schools, colleges, hospitals, and the military—even in proportion to our membership, we do not. One barrier to effectiveness in community ministry is the lack of a common understanding of the place of community ministry in congregational ecclesiology.

Reaching out to the larger public community has been an essential part of Unitarianism and Universalism. UUA President Peter Morales has recently challenged us to think deeply about community ministry in his initiative "Congregations and Beyond." He notes, "An increasing percentage of seminarians choose a community ministry rather than parish ministry. They see themselves as having a vocation for ministry, but not for parish ministry. Our ministry extends to prisons, hospitals, the military and organizations that seek to build a more compassionate and just world." This recognition is an invitation to our association to invest resources to expand the visibility of chaplaincy and its contributions to our movement, because chaplains have particular capacities that are underutilized by our association.

UU chaplains as spiritual theologians and multifaith brokers

In settings that are increasingly multifaith, generic chaplaincy is becoming the norm, with chaplains journeying alongside people of different faith groups. The wide-ranging liberal theological constructs of Unitarian Universalism are providing models for the discipline. UU chaplains are also spiritual theologians who "do theology"—who reflect theologically on encounters with people, for whom there are more questions than answers. Not only are chaplains "being theologians" as they journey alongside people, they are "doing theology" when they reflect critically on these encounters.

UU chaplains as spiritual curators

Everyone, we might say, believes in someone or something. Everyone is committed in some way to an idea or philosophy. UU chaplains are in the unique position of being able to understand this and aid a person in their faith journey, whatever that may be. As a faith community that encourages its members to develop their own robust theology based on experience, reason, and spirit, we are comfortable with the increasing religious ambiguity in our culture. As chaplains we do not provide simplistic platitudes, blessings, and prayers. Instead, we journey with people and address the particular needs of their narrative. As Unitarian Universalists, we are able to draw on a wide variety of spiritual, religious, and philosophical resources to assist care seekers as they affirm their current beliefs or explore new possibilities for comfort and community.

Unitarian Universalist chaplains as interpreters

Chaplains must be well versed in the variety of spiritual texts found in our culture in order to be able to understand the many languages of spiritual pain that care seekers may use. The training and sensitivity that is required for this are expected of UU ministers, who are required to study world religions and are accustomed to functioning among people who utilize a variety of texts and traditions. Chaplains also work across disciplines, and it is critical that we understand the languages of different groups: doctors and nurses; administrators and assistants; Unitarian Universalists, members of other faiths, and members of none; patients and families. Since Unitarian Universalists are comfortable with the marriage of medical science and spirituality, we are frequently called to translate for patients who do not understand the medical jargon or for staff who do not understand patients' spiritual pain.

Unitarian Universalist chaplains as prophetic voices

Sometimes Unitarian Universalist chaplains have a distinctive role as prophetic voices, standing up in the face of injustice or wrongs. They can do so by arbitrating between people, such as between staff, patients, and families. In fact, many problems and scandals have been averted because a chaplain has been in the right place at the right time. The unique training of UU ministers makes them well suited to mediate and intervene when social injustice or oppression mean that care seekers may be poorly served or not attain what they seek.

The UUA includes almost two hundred fellowshipped chaplains, and this volume shows that they are functioning in dynamic and generative settings. As Unitarian Universalists, they are putting flesh on our Principles and Purposes in the larger world.

Benediction

Chaplains continue to show up . . .

We show up to hold hands when you get the news that you have been both wanting and dreading.

We show up to stand in those liminal spaces with you that are void of clarity and pregnant with possibilities.

We show up at your cell with a card to remind you that the free world has not forgotten you.

We show up as you gather the shards and shreds of your past relationships when you relapse for the fifth time.

We show up when you can't get that sound of the IED out of your ears or the images out of your mind.

We show up at the bedside for the beauty and poignancy of dying and living side by side in a community of care.

We will continue to show up because we care about your search for meaning, truth, and healing.

About the Contributors

Emily Brault spent three years as a chaplain with the Minnesota Department of Corrections and has been in the Oregon system since 2004. Her experiences as a human being, academic, and chaplain actively shape her vision of what a just society looks, feels, and acts like. Her highest hope is that we are all part of the solution and that there is more chocolate for everyone.

Keith Goheen, a Board Certified Chaplain, is a chaplain at Beebe Healthcare in Lewes, Delaware, where he specializes in end-of-life care, trauma, and crisis support. He was ordained by the First Universalist Church of Orange (Massachusetts). His practice teaches that our souls are made from and for stories, and that love's story prevails.

Mandy Goheen is the director of prison ministry at the Church of the Larger Fellowship. She is a candidate for the Unitarian Universalist ministry, in her final semester at Starr King School for the Ministry. Her spouse serves in the Air Force, stationed in Montgomery, Alabama. They live in a big, active household with four of their six adopted children and two dogs.

Karen L. Hutt has been an educator for thirty years and is currently serving as the certified Association of Clinical Pastoral Education supervisor at the University of Minnesota Medical

Center. She is committed to the training of chaplains for the twenty-first century and has developed innovative curriculum materials for her students to learn the practical skills required to be successful in pluralistic, institutional settings. She is a creator, innovator, and generational bridge-builder.

Rebekah C. Ingram is a chaplain at Beth Israel Deaconess Medical Center in Boston, where she provides spiritual care, with a focus on oncology, to patients and families throughout the hospital. She is also a member of the outpatient palliative care team. She became a Board Certified Chaplain in 2011. In addition to serving in hospitals, she has worked at hospice facilities. She lives in Walpole, Massachusetts, with her spouse and their son.

Xolani Kacela is a Unitarian Universalist minister serving as a chaplain in the District of Columbia Air National Guard. He has deployed four times, including Operation Iraqi Freedom and Hurricane Katrina Relief. He serves as assistant minister at Eno River Unitarian Universalist Fellowship in Durham, North Carolina, and as adjunct faculty at Meadville Lombard Theological School. He is married to Tamara.

Cynthia Kane was ordained in May 1997 and commissioned by the Navy in August 2001. She has ministered in various institutions: Guantanamo Bay detention center, civilian hospitals, Navy aircraft carriers, Coast Guard cutters, and Marine units. Her greatest achievements are her marriage, her two children's births, and parenting three boys. She gratefully lives in the intersection of three worlds: ministry, military, and motherhood.

Holly Anne Lux-Sullivan works as a hospice chaplain in central North Carolina, ministering to terminally ill patients and their families in their homes. A former newspaper journalist, she came to ministry through her volunteer work with the HIV/AIDS communities in Athens, Ohio, and Greensboro, North Carolina. She shares life with her husband, Kevin, and their retired racing greyhounds.

Jane Ellen Mauldin has served in Unitarian Universalist ministry for more than thirty-five years. As a Board Certified Chaplain in a busy New Orleans hospital, she laughs, cries, and prays frequently. A mother and grandmother, her soul is fed by her fabulous family, regular meditation practice, and the amazing patients and hospital staff with whom she spends her days.

Nathan Mesnikoff is director of spiritual care at Memorial Hospital: University of Colorado Health in Colorado Springs. As chair of the hospital's medical ethics committee he continues to work with patients, families, and staff facing complex challenges. He is the affiliated community minister for High Plains Church Unitarian Universalist in Colorado Springs, Colorado. He and his family live close to the mountains they love and enjoy hiking and backpacking in Colorado's beautiful wilderness.

Lisa Presley is a life-long Unitarian Universalist who has served as an interim and settled minister. She currently serves as congregational life consultant for the MidAmerica Region of the Unitarian Universalist Association. She served for a decade as a police chaplain in her community, a suburb of Detroit. It was some of the most transforming ministry she has performed.

Kathy Riegelman is a Board Certified Chaplain and serves as a hospital chaplain in Kansas City, Missouri. She has served on the Greater Kansas City Interfaith Council since 1999 and as an adjunct faculty member at Unity Institute. She is the author of the Unitarian Universalist chapter in *The Essential Guide to Religious Traditions and Spirituality for Health Care Providers*, published by Radcliffe Medical Press.

Barbara Stevens, a Board Certified Chaplain, specializes in addiction and mental health chaplaincy. She worked for seven years in the Chemical Dependency Unit at Providence Health Services in Portland, Oregon. Now at Kaiser Hospital, she sees not only general hospital patients, but also patients on the mental health and addiction units. She is the minister of the Universalist Recovery Church, a spiritual community for people in recovery.

Karen B. Taliesin is a Board Certified Chaplain who has been a chaplain at Seattle Children's Hospital since 2002. For more than twenty-eight years, she has worked with dying and bereft patients and families, with an emphasis on hospital staff care. She consults and teaches in the areas of spiritual care, grief and bereavement, compassion fatigue, trauma stewardship, resiliency, and mindfulness.

Andrew Tripp has several years of experience in hospital and hospice chaplaincy, working in culturally, socioeconomically, and religiously diverse settings. His chaplaincy practice includes significant work with patients and their families dealing with dementia. His academic work focuses on the intersection of pastoral care and social ethics, including published articles in the journal *Theopoetics*.